DETERRENCE
AND THE
DEATH PENALTY

Committee on Deterrence and the Death Penalty

Daniel S. Nagin and John V. Pepper, *Editors*

Committee on Law and Justice

Division of Behavioral and Social Sciences and Education

NATIONAL RESEARCH COUNCIL
OF THE NATIONAL ACADEMIES

THE NATIONAL ACADEMIES PRESS
Washington, D.C.
www.nap.edu

THE NATIONAL ACADEMIES PRESS • 500 Fifth Street, NW • Washington, DC 20001

NOTICE: The project that is the subject of this report was approved by the Governing Board of the National Research Council, whose members are drawn from the councils of the National Academy of Sciences, the National Academy of Engineering, and the Institute of Medicine. The members of the committee responsible for the report were chosen for their special competences and with regard for appropriate balance.

This study was supported by Grant Number 2010-IJ-CX-0018 from the National Institute of Justice, Grant Number TRF09-01115 from the Tides Foundation, and the Proteus Action League (grant not numbered). Any opinions, findings, conclusions, or recommendations expressed in this publication are those of the author(s) and do not necessarily reflect the views of the organizations or agencies that provided support for the project.

International Standard Book Number-13:   978-0-309-25416-8
International Standard Book Number-10:   0-309-25416-7

Additional copies of this report are available from the National Academies Press, 500 Fifth Street, NW, Keck 360, Washington, DC 20001; (800) 624-6242 or (202) 334-3313; http://www.nap.edu.

Suggested citation: National Research Council. (2012). *Deterrence and the Death Penalty*. Committee on Deterrence and the Death Penalty, Daniel S. Nagin and John V. Pepper, Eds. Committee on Law and Justice, Division of Behavioral and Social Sciences and Education. Washington, DC: The National Academies Press.

THE NATIONAL ACADEMIES
Advisers to the Nation on Science, Engineering, and Medicine

The **National Academy of Sciences** is a private, nonprofit, self-perpetuating society of distinguished scholars engaged in scientific and engineering research, dedicated to the furtherance of science and technology and to their use for the general welfare. Upon the authority of the charter granted to it by the Congress in 1863, the Academy has a mandate that requires it to advise the federal government on scientific and technical matters. Dr. Ralph J. Cicerone is president of the National Academy of Sciences.

The **National Academy of Engineering** was established in 1964, under the charter of the National Academy of Sciences, as a parallel organization of outstanding engineers. It is autonomous in its administration and in the selection of its members, sharing with the National Academy of Sciences the responsibility for advising the federal government. The National Academy of Engineering also sponsors engineering programs aimed at meeting national needs, encourages education and research, and recognizes the superior achievements of engineers. Dr. Charles M. Vest is president of the National Academy of Engineering.

The **Institute of Medicine** was established in 1970 by the National Academy of Sciences to secure the services of eminent members of appropriate professions in the examination of policy matters pertaining to the health of the public. The Institute acts under the responsibility given to the National Academy of Sciences by its congressional charter to be an adviser to the federal government and, upon its own initiative, to identify issues of medical care, research, and education. Dr. Harvey V. Fineberg is president of the Institute of Medicine.

The **National Research Council** was organized by the National Academy of Sciences in 1916 to associate the broad community of science and technology with the Academy's purposes of furthering knowledge and advising the federal government. Functioning in accordance with general policies determined by the Academy, the Council has become the principal operating agency of both the National Academy of Sciences and the National Academy of Engineering in providing services to the government, the public, and the scientific and engineering communities. The Council is administered jointly by both Academies and the Institute of Medicine. Dr. Ralph J. Cicerone and Dr. Charles M. Vest are chair and vice chair, respectively, of the National Research Council.

www.national-academies.org

IN MEMORIAM

James Q. Wilson
1931-2012

"I've tried to follow the facts wherever they land."

This report is dedicated to James Q. Wilson for his long service to the National Research Council, his influential career of scholarship and public service, and his unblinking commitment to the principle that science requires us to interpret the evidence as it is, not as we want it to be.

Preface

More than three decades ago, in *Deterrence and Incapacitation: Estimating the Effects of Criminal Sanctions on Crime Rates,* the National Research Council (NRC) (1978, p. 9) concluded that "available studies provide no useful evidence on the deterrent effect of capital punishment." That report was issued 2 years after the Supreme Court decision in *Gregg v. Georgia* ended a 4-year moratorium on execution in the United States. In the 35 years since the publication of that report, especially in recent years, a considerable number of post-*Gregg* studies have attempted to estimate the effect of the legal status or the actual implementation of the death penalty on homicide rates. Those studies have reached widely varying conclusions.

Against this background, the NRC formed the Committee on Deterrence and the Death Penalty to address whether the available evidence provides a reasonable basis for drawing conclusions about the magnitude of the effect of capital punishment on homicide rates. At a workshop on April 28-29, 2011, workshop papers commissioned by the committee (which will be published in a special issue of the *Journal of Quantitative Criminology*) were presented and discussed by their authors: Robert J. Apel, University at Albany, State University of New York; Aaron Chalfin, University of California, Berkeley; Chao Fu, University of Wisconsin–Madison; Justin McCrary, University of California, Berkeley; Salvador Navarro, University of Western Ontario, Ontario, Canada; John V. Pepper, University of Virginia; and Steven Raphael, University of California, Berkeley. The workshop also included comments on the presentations by Jeffrey Grogger, University of Chicago; Guido Imbens, Harvard University; Kenneth C. Land, Duke

University; Christopher Sims, Princeton University; and Justin Wolfers, University of Pennsylvania.

The committee appreciates the contributions of these presenters and those who commented on them to the development of its report. In addition, John V. Pepper provided invaluable assistance to the committee throughout its deliberations. The work of staff members from the Committee on Law and Justice of the NRC facilitated the committee's work in many ways. Thanks are due to Jane L. Ross, study director; Keiko Ono, senior program associate; Carol Hayes, Christine Mirzayan fellow; and Barbara Boyd, administrative coordinator.

Many individuals at the NRC assisted the committee. We thank Kirsten Sampson-Snyder, who shepherded the report through the NRC review process, Eugenia Grohman, who edited the draft report, and Yvonne Wise, for processing the report through final production.

This report has been reviewed in draft form by individuals chosen for their diverse perspectives and technical expertise, in accordance with procedures approved by the NRC's Report Review Committee. The purpose of this independent review is to provide candid and critical comments that will assist the institution in making its published report as sound as possible and to ensure that the report meets institutional standards for objectivity, evidence, and responsiveness to the study charge. The review comments and draft manuscript remain confidential to protect the integrity of the deliberative process. We thank the following individuals for their review of this report: John Donohue, III, Stanford Law School, Stanford University; Andrew Gelman, Department of Statistics and Department of Political Science, Columbia University; Kenneth C. Land, Department of Sociology, Duke University; Candice Odgers, School of Social Ecology, University of California, Irvine; Ricardo Reis, Department of Economics, Columbia University; Greg Ridgeway, RAND Safety and Justice Program, RAND Center on Quality Policing, RAND Corporation; Robert J. Sampson, Department of Sociology, Harvard University; Dick Thornburgh, Counsel, K&L Gates, LLP, and former Attorney General of the United States; Petra E. Todd, Department of Economics, University of Pennsylvania; and Michael Tonry, School of Law, University of Minnesota, Minneapolis.

Although the reviewers listed above have provided many constructive comments and suggestions, they were not asked to endorse the conclusions or recommendations nor did they see the final draft of the report before its release. The review of this report was overseen by Gary LaFree, National Consortium for the Study of Terrorism and Responses to Terrorism, University of Maryland, and John T. Monahan, University of Virginia Law School. Appointed by the NRC, they were responsible for making certain that an independent examination of this report was carried out in accordance with institutional procedures and that all review comments were carefully considered. Responsibility for the final content of this report rests entirely with the authoring committee and the institution.

This report is dedicated to James Q. Wilson. Jim was a valued member of this and many other NRC committees on which he served over his long and influential career. Jim's contributions to scholarship and public service will stand as enduring testimony to the power of his intellect. He was a quiet but forceful proponent for balanced and clear-minded assessment of the evidence. I first met Jim in my role as a staff member of the 1978 NRC committee that resulted in report *Deterrence and Incapacitation: Estimating the Effect of Criminal Sanctions on Crime Rates.* I was deeply impressed by the clarity of his thought and gift for communication. He served as a role model for me ever since. I was thus especially honored that he agreed to serve on this committee, which was greatly aided by his constructive participation throughout our deliberations.

Daniel S. Nagin, *Chair*
Committee on Deterrence and the Death Penalty

Contents

SUMMARY   1
    Shortcomings in Existing Research, 4
      Specification of the Sanction Regime for Homicide, 4
      Potential Murderers' Perceptions of and Responses to
        Capital Punishment, 5
    Strong and Unverifiable Assumptions, 6
    Next Steps for Research, 7
    References, 8

1   INTRODUCTION   9
    The Current Debate, 9
    Committee Charge and Scope of Work, 11
    References, 14

2   CAPITAL PUNISHMENT IN THE POST-*GREGG* ERA   15
    Executions and Death Sentences Over Time, 15
    Use of the Death Penalty, 20
    References, 26

3   DETERMINING THE DETERRENT EFFECT OF
    CAPITAL PUNISHMENT: KEY ISSUES   27
    Concepts of Deterrence, 28
    Sanction Regimes, 32

Data Issues, 36
Variations in Murder Rates, 37
Reciprocal Effects Between Homicide Rates and
    Sanction Regimes, 41
Summary, 43
References, 44

4   PANEL STUDIES   47
Panel Studies Reviewed, 48
    Methods Used: Overview, 48
    The Studies, Their Characteristics, and the Effects Found, 49
Specifying the Expected Cost of Committing a Capital
    Homicide: $f(Z_{it})$, 54
Model Assumptions, 63
    Benefits of Random Assignment, 64
    Fixed Effect Regression Model, 65
    Instrumental Variables, 66
    Homogeneity, 68
Conclusion, 70
References, 71

5   TIME-SERIES STUDIES   75
Basic Conceptual Issues, 76
    Execution Event Studies, 76
    Studies of Deviations from Fitted Trends, 78
Vector Autoregressions, 82
    Evidence Under Existing Criminal Sanction Regimes, 82
        Granger Causality and Causality as Treatment Response, 86
        Choice of Variables in VAR Studies, 88
    Inferences Under Alternative Sanction Regimes, 89
Event Studies, 90
Time-Series Regressions, 92
Cross-Polity Comparisons, 94
Conclusions, 97
References, 99

6   CHALLENGES TO IDENTIFYING DETERRENT EFFECTS   101
Data on Sanction Regimes, 104
Perceptions of Sanction Risks, 105
    Measurement of Perceptions, 107
    Inference on Perceptions from Homicide Rates Following
    Executions, 110

Identifying Effects: Feedbacks and Unobserved Confounders, 111
   Feedback Effects, 111
   Omitted Variables, 112
   The Equilibrium Effect, 113
Addressing Model Uncertainty with Weaker Assumptions, 115
   Model Averaging, 116
   Partial Identification, 119
References, 121

Appendix: Biographical Sketches of Committee Members and Staff   125

Summary

In 1976, the Supreme Court decision in *Gregg v. Georgia* (428 U.S. 153) ended the 4-year moratorium on executions that had resulted from its 1972 decision in *Furman v. Georgia* (408 U.S. 238). In the immediate aftermath of *Gregg*, an earlier report of the National Research Council (NRC) reviewed the evidence relating to the deterrent effect of the death penalty that had been gathered through the mid-1970s. That review was highly critical of the earlier research and concluded (National Research Council, 1978, p. 9) that "available studies provide no useful evidence on the deterrent effect of capital punishment."

During the 35 years since *Gregg*, and particularly in the past decade, many additional studies have renewed the attempt to estimate the effect of capital punishment on homicide rates. Most researchers have used post-*Gregg* data from the United States to examine the statistical association between homicide rates and the legal status, the actual implementation of the death penalty, or both. The studies have reached widely varying, even contradictory, conclusions. Some studies conclude that executions save large numbers of lives; others conclude that executions actually increase homicides; and still others conclude that executions have no effect on homicide rate. Commentary on the scientific validity of the findings has sometimes been acrimonious. The Committee on Deterrence and the Death Penalty was convened against this backdrop of conflicting claims about the effect of capital punishment on homicide rates. The committee addressed three main questions laid out in its charge:

1. Does the available evidence provide a reasonable basis for drawing conclusions about the magnitude of capital punishment's effect on homicide rates?
2. Are there differences among the extant analyses that provide a basis for resolving the differences in findings? Are the differences in findings due to inherent limitations in the data? Are there existing statistical methods and/or theoretical perspectives that have yet to be applied that can better address the deterrence question? Are the limitations of existing evidence reflective of a lack of information about the social, economic, and political underpinnings of homicide rates and/or the administration of capital punishment that first must be resolved before the deterrent effect of capital punishment can be determined?
3. Do potential remedies to shortcomings in the evidence on the deterrent effect of capital punishment have broader applicability for research on the deterrent effect of noncapital sanctions?

CONCLUSION AND RECOMMENDATION: The committee concludes that research to date on the effect of capital punishment on homicide is not informative about whether capital punishment decreases, increases, or has no effect on homicide rates. Therefore, the committee recommends that these studies not be used to inform deliberations requiring judgments about the effect of the death penalty on homicide. Consequently, claims that research demonstrates that capital punishment decreases or increases the homicide rate by a specified amount or has no effect on the homicide rate should not influence policy judgments about capital punishment.

The committee was disappointed to reach the conclusion that research conducted in the 30 years since the earlier NRC report has not sufficiently advanced knowledge to allow a conclusion, however qualified, about the effect of the death penalty on homicide rates. Yet this is our conclusion. Some studies play the useful role, either intentionally or not, of demonstrating the fragility of claims to have or not to have found deterrent effects. However, even these studies suffer from two intrinsic shortcomings that severely limit what can be learned from them about the effect of the death penalty—as it has actually been administered in the United States in the past 35 years—on the death penalty.

Properly understood, the relevant question about the deterrent effect of capital punishment is the differential or marginal deterrent effect of execution over the deterrent effect of other available or commonly used penalties, specifically, a lengthy prison sentence or one of life without the possibility of parole. One major deficiency in all the existing studies is that none specify the noncapital sanction components of the sanction regime for the punishment of homicide. Another major deficiency is the use of incomplete or implausible models of potential murderers' perceptions of and response to the capital punishment component of a sanction regime. Without this basic information, it is impossible to draw credible findings about the effect of the death penalty on homicide.

Commentary on research findings often pits studies claiming to find statistically significant deterrent effects against those finding no statistically significant effects, with the latter studies sometimes interpreted as implying that there is no deterrent effect. A fundamental point of logic about hypothesis testing is that failure to reject a null hypothesis does not imply that the null hypothesis is correct.

Our mandate was not to assess whether competing hypotheses about the existence of marginal deterrence from capital punishment are plausible, but simply to assess whether the empirical studies that we have reviewed provide scientifically valid evidence. In its deliberations and in this report, the committee has made a concerted effort not to approach this question with a prior assumption about deterrence. Having reviewed the research that purports to provide useful evidence for or against the hypothesis that the death penalty affects homicide rates, we conclude that it does not provide such evidence.

A lack of evidence is not evidence for or against the hypothesis. Hence, the committee does not construe its conclusion that the existing studies are uninformative as favoring one side or the other side in the long-standing debate about deterrence and the death penalty. The committee also emphasizes that deterrence is but one of many considerations relevant to rendering a judgment on whether the death penalty is good public policy.

Even though the scholarly evidence on the deterrent effect of capital punishment is too weak to guide decisions, this does not mean that people should have no views on capital punishment. Judgment about whether there is a deterrent effect is still relevant to policy, but that judgment should not be justified based on evidence from existing research on capital punishment's effect on homicide. Just as important, the committee did not investigate the moral arguments for or against capital punishment or the empirical evidence on whether capital punishment is administered in a nondiscriminatory and consistent fashion. Nor did it investigate whether the risk of mistaken execution is acceptably small or how the cost of administering the death penalty compares to other sanction alternatives. All of these issues are relevant to making a judgment about whether the death penalty is good public policy.

Our charge was also limited to assessing the evidence on the deterrent effect of the death penalty on murder, not the deterrent effect of noncapital sanctions on crime more generally. Our negative conclusion on the informativeness of the evidence on the former issue should not be construed as extending to the latter issue because the committee did not review the very large body of evidence on the deterrent effect of noncapital sanctions.

SHORTCOMINGS IN EXISTING RESEARCH

The post-*Gregg* studies are usefully divided into two categories based on the type of data analyzed. One category, which we call *panel data studies,* analyzes sets of states or counties measured over time, usually from about 1970 to 2000. These studies relate homicide rates to variations over time and across states or counties in the legal status of capital punishment and/or the frequency of executions. The second category, which we call *time-series studies*, generally studies only a single geographic unit. The geographic unit may be as large as a nation or as small as a city. These studies usually examine whether there are short-term changes in homicide rates in that geographic unit in the aftermath of an execution.

As noted above, research on the effect of capital punishment on homicide suffers from two fundamental flaws that make them uninformative about the effect of capital punishment on homicide rates: they do not specify the noncapital sanction components of the sanction regime for the punishment of homicide, and they use incomplete or implausible models of potential murderers' perceptions of and response to the capital punishment component of a sanction regime. In addition, the existing studies use strong and unverifiable assumptions to identify the effects of capital punishment on homicides.

Specification of the Sanction Regime for Homicide

The sanction regime for homicide comprises both the capital and noncapital sanctioning options that are available for its punishment and the policies governing the administration of these options. The relevant question regarding the deterrent effect of capital punishment is the differential deterrent effect of execution in comparison with the deterrent effect of other available or commonly used penalties. We emphasize "differential" because it is important to recognize that even in states that make the most intense use of capital punishment, most convicted murderers are not sentenced to death but to a lengthy prison sentence—often life without the possibility of parole.

None of the studies that we reviewed (both those using a panel approach and those using time-series approaches) accounted for the severity of noncapital sanctions in their analyses. As discussed in Chapters 4 and 6, there are sound reasons to expect that the severity of the noncapital sanctions for homicide varies systematically with the availability of capital punishment, the intensity of use of capital punishment, or both. For example, the political culture of a state may affect the frequency of the use of capital punishment and also the severity of noncapital sanctions for homicide. Thus, any effect that these noncapital sanctions have on the homicide rate may contaminate any estimated effect of capital punishment.

Potential Murderers' Perceptions of and Responses to Capital Punishment

A by-product of the absence of consideration of the noncapital component of the sanction regime is that no studies consider how the capital and noncapital components of a regime combine in affecting the behavior of potential murderers. Only the capital component of the sanction regime has been studied, and this in itself shows both a serious conceptual flaw and a serious data flaw in the entire body of research.

Several factors make the attempts by the panel studies to specify the capital component of state sanctions regimes uninterpretable. First, the findings are very sensitive to the way the risk of execution is specified. Second, there is no logical basis for resolving disagreements about how this risk should be measured.

Much of the panel research simply assumes that potential murderers respond to the objective risk of execution. There are significant complexities in computing this risk even for a well-informed researcher, let alone for a potential murderer. Among these complexities are that only 15 percent of people who have been sentenced to death since 1976 have actually been executed and a large fraction of death sentences are subsequently reversed. None of the measures that are used in the research have been shown to be a better measure of the risk of execution than any others. Thus, even if one assumes that a potential murderer's perceived risk corresponds to the actual risk, there is no basis for arbitrating the competing claims about what is the "right" risk measure.

The committee is also skeptical that potential murderers can possibly estimate the objective risk, whatever it is. Hence, there is good reason to believe that perceived risk deviates from the objective risk. The research does not address how potential murderers' perceptions of capital punishment—and, more generally, noncapital sanction risks—are formed.

The time-series studies come in many forms—studies of a single execution event, studies of many events, and studies with a cross-polity dimension—but a common feature of the studies is that none of them attempts to specify even the capital component of the overall sanction regime. This is a crucial shortcoming and is exemplified in the time-series analyses that examine the association between deviations of number of executions from a fitted trend line and deviations of homicides from a fitted trend line.

For potential murderers to possibly be responsive to deviations from the execution trend line, they have to be attentive to it. The studies are silent on two key questions: (1) Why are potential murderers attentive to the trend line in the number of executions? (2) Why do they respond to deviations from the trend line?

If time-series analyses find that homicide rates are not responsive to such deviations, it may be that potential murderers are responding to the trend line in executions but not to deviations from it. For example, a rising trend in the number of executions might be perceived as signaling a toughening of the sanction regime, which might deter potential murderers. Alternatively, if a time-series analysis finds that homicide rates are responsive to such deviations, the question is why? One possibility is that potential murderers interpret the deviations as new information about the intensity of the application of capital punishment—that is, they perceive a change in the part of the sanction regime relating to application of capital punishment. If so, a deviation from the execution trend line may cause potential murderers to alter their perceptions of the future course of the trend line, which in turn may change their behavior.

Yet, even accepting this idea, a basic question persists. Why should the trend lines fit by researchers coincide with the perceptions of potential murderers about trends in executions? Because there are no studies that include empirical analyses on the question of how potential murderers perceive the risk of sanctions, there is no basis for assuming that the trend line specified by researchers corresponds to the trend line (if any) that is perceived by potential murderers. If researchers and potential murderers do not perceive trends the same way, then time-series analyses do not correctly identify what potential murderers perceive as deviations. Because of this basic flaw in the research, the committee has no basis for assessing whether the findings of time-series studies reflect a real effect of executions on homicides or are artifacts of models that incorrectly specify how deviations from a trend line cause potential murderers to update their forecasts of the future course of executions.

Strong and Unverifiable Assumptions

To obtain a single estimate that specifies the effect of capital punishment on homicide, researchers invariably rely on a range of strong and unverified assumptions. In part (as discussed above), this reflects the lack of basic information on the relevant sanction regimes for homicide and the associated perceptions of risk. None of the studies accounts for the noncapital component of the sanction regime, and potential murderers' risk perceptions are assumed to depend on observable frequencies of arrest, conviction, and execution. The ad hoc choices of alternative models of risk perceptions lead to very different inferences on the effects of capital punishment, and none of them is inherently any more justifiable than any other.

Additional data and research on sanction regimes and risk perceptions may serve to reduce this form of model uncertainty. However, even if these uncertainties are fully reconciled, a more fundamental problem is that the outcomes of counterfactual sanction policies are unobservable. That is, there is no way to determine what would have occurred if a given state had a different sanction regime. In light of this observational problem, the available data cannot reveal the effect of capital punishment itself since the policy-relevant question is whether capital punishment deters homicides relative to other sanction regimes. That is, the data alone cannot reveal what the homicide rate in a state without (with) a capital punishment regime would have been had the state (not) had such a regime.

The standard procedure in capital punishment research has been to impose sufficiently strong assumptions to yield definitive findings on deterrence. For example, a common assumption is that sanctions are random across states or years, as they would be if sanctions had been randomly assigned in an experiment. Another common assumption is that the response of criminality to sanctions is homogeneous across states and years. Some studies use instrumental variables to identify deterrent effects, but this requires yet other assumptions. The use of strong assumptions hides the problem that the study of deterrence is plagued by model uncertainty and that many of the assumptions used in the research lack credibility.

NEXT STEPS FOR RESEARCH

The earlier NRC committee concluded that it was "skeptical that the death penalty [as practiced in the United States] can ever be subjected to the kind of statistical analysis that would validly establish the presence or absence of a deterrent effect" (National Research Council, 1978, p. 62). The present committee is not so pessimistic and offers several recommendations for addressing the shortcomings in research to date on capital punishment. They include

1. collection of the data required for a more complete specification of both the capital and noncapital components of the sanction regime for murder;
2. research on how potential murderers perceive the sanction regime for murder; and
3. use of methods that makes less strong and more credible assumptions to identify or bound the effect of capital punishment on homicides.

In addition, the committee suggests research on how the presence of capital punishment in a sanctions regime affects the administration of the regime and how the homicide rate affects the statutory definition of the sanction regime and its administration.

The committee does not expect that advances in new data on sanction regimes and obtaining knowledge of sanctions risk perceptions will come quickly or easily. However, data collection on the noncapital component of the sanction regime need not be entirely complete to be useful. Moreover, even if research on perceptions of the risk of capital punishment cannot resolve all major issues, some progress would be an important step forward.

The ultimate success of the research may depend on the specific question that is addressed. Questions of interest include

- if or how the legal status of the death penalty affects homicide rates,
- if or how the intensity of use of the death penalty affects homicide rates, and
- if or how executions affect homicide rates in the short run.

Some but not all of these questions may be informed by successful application of the committee's suggested lines of research.

Although evaluation of research on the deterrent effect of noncapital sanctions was not part of the committee's charge, we note that the methods and approaches used to study capital and noncapital sanction effects on crime overlap. We were charged with making suggestions for advancing research on the latter issue. Thus, the research and data collection suggestions above are framed in the broader context of research on the effect on crime rates of both capital and noncapital sanctions.

We think this aspect of our charge is particularly important. Although capital punishment is a highly contentious public policy issue, policies on prison sanctions and their enforcement are the most important components of the nation's response to crime. Thus, even if the research agenda we outline is not ultimately successful in illuminating some aspects of the effect of capital punishment on homicide, advancing knowledge on the crime prevention effects of noncapital sanctions and their enforcement can make major contributions to important policy issues.

REFERENCE

National Research Council. (1978). *Deterrence and Incapacitation: Estimating the Effects of Criminal Sanctions on Crime Rates.* Panel on Research on Deterrent and Incapacitative Effects. A. Blumstein, J. Cohen, and D. Nagin (Eds.), Committee on Research on Law Enforcement and Criminal Justice. Assembly of Behavioral and Social Sciences. Washington, DC: National Academy Press.

1

Introduction

In 1976 the Supreme Court decision *Gregg v. Georgia* (428 U.S. 153) ended the 4-year moratorium on executions that had resulted from its 1972 decision in *Furman v. Georgia* (408 U.S. 238). In *Furman* the Court had ruled that the death penalty, as then administered in the United States, constituted cruel and unusual punishment in violation of the Eighth Amendment to the Constitution. Then, in *Gregg*, it had ruled that the death penalty is not, in all circumstances, cruel and unusual punishment, thereby opening the way for states to revise their capital punishment statutes to conform to the requirements of *Gregg*.

In the immediate aftermath of *Gregg*, a National Research Council report reviewed the evidence relating to the deterrent effect of the death penalty that had been published through the mid-1970s. That review was highly critical of the available research, concluding (1978, p. 9):

> The flaws in the earlier analyses finding no effect and the sensitivity of the more recent analysis to minor variations in model specification and the serious temporal instability of the results lead the panel to conclude that available studies provide no useful evidence on the deterrent effect of capital punishment.

THE CURRENT DEBATE

During the 35 years since *Gregg*, and particularly in the past decade, many studies have renewed the attempt to estimate the effect of capital punishment on homicide rates. Most researchers have used post-*Gregg* data from the United States to examine the statistical association between homicide rates and the legal status or the actual implementation of the death penalty.

The studies have reached widely varying, even contradictory, conclusions, and commentary on the findings has sometimes been acrimonious. Some researchers have concluded that deterrent effects are large and robust across datasets and model specifications. For example, Dezhbakhsh, Rubin, and Shepherd (2003, p. 344) concluded that:

> Our results suggest that capital punishment has a strong deterrent effect; each execution results, on average, in eighteen fewer murders with a margin of error of plus or minus ten. Tests show that results are not driven by tougher sentencing laws and are robust to many alternative specifications.

Similarly, Mocan and Gittings (2003, p. 453) stated the following:

> The results show that each additional execution decreases homicides by about five, and each additional commutation increases homicides by the same amount, while an additional removal from death row generates one additional murder.

In 2004 testimony before Congress, Shepherd (2004, p. 1) summarized this line of evidence on the deterrent effect of capital punishment as follows:

> Recent research on the relationship between capital punishment and crime has created a strong consensus among economists that capital punishment deters crime.

However, the claims that the evidence shows a substantial deterrent effect have been vigorously challenged. Kovandzic, Vieraitis, and Boots (2009, p. 803) concluded that:

> Employing well-known econometric procedures for panel data analysis, our results provide no empirical support for the argument that the existence or application of the death penalty deters prospective offenders from committing homicide . . . policymakers should refrain from justifying its use by claiming that it is a deterrent to homicide and should consider less costly, more effective ways of addressing crime.

Others do not go so far as to claim that there is no deterrent effect, but instead argue that the findings supporting a deterrent effect are fragile, not robust. Donohue and Wolfers (2005, p. 794) reanalyzed several of the data sets used by the authors who claimed to have found robust deterrent effects and concluded that:

> We find that the existing evidence for deterrence is surprisingly fragile, and even small changes in specifications yield dramatically different re-

sults. Our key insight is that the death penalty—at least as it has been implemented in the United States since *Gregg* ended the moratorium on executions—is applied so rarely that the number of homicides it can plausibly have caused or deterred cannot be reliably disentangled from the large year-to year changes in the homicide rate caused by other factors.

Berk (2005, p. 328) reached a similar conclusion:

> ... the results raise serious questions about whether anything useful about the deterrent value of the death penalty can ever be learned from an observational study with the data that are likely to be available.

Not surprisingly, the criticisms of the research claiming to have found deterrent effects have generated defenses of the research findings and the methodologies used, as well as counterclaims about the deficiencies in the methods used by the critics. For instance, in response to the Kovandzic, Vieraitis, and Boots (2009) claim of no deterrent effect, Rubin (2009, p. 858) argued that:

> the weight of the evidence as well as the theoretical predictions both argue for deterrence, and econometrically flawed studies such as this article are insufficient to overthrow this presumption.

In response to Donohue and Wolfers (2005, 2009), Zimmerman (2009, p. 396) argued that:

> This paper shows that many of D&W's [Donohue and Wolfers] criticisms of Zimmerman's original work do not hold up under scrutiny, and other authors have also rebutted D&W's criticisms of their research.

Beyond disagreement about whether the research evidence shows a deterrent effect of capital punishment, some researchers claim to have found a brutalization effect from state-sanctioned executions such that capital punishment actually *increases* homicide rates (see, e.g., Cochran and Chamlin, 2000; Thomson, 1999). Evidence in support of a brutalization effect is mostly the work of sociologists, but it is notable that in her latter work Shepherd also concluded that brutalization effects may be present (Shepherd, 2005).

COMMITTEE CHARGE AND SCOPE OF WORK

The Committee on Deterrence and the Death Penalty was organized against this backdrop of conflicting claims about the effect of capital punishment on homicide rates, with the following charge:

This study will assess the evidence on the deterrent effect of the death penalty—whether the threat of execution prevents homicides. The focus will be on studies completed since an earlier National Research Council assessment (National Research Council, 1978). A major objective of this study is to evaluate underlying reasons for the differing conclusions in more recent empirical studies about the effects of the legal status and actual practice of the death penalty on criminal homicide rates. The committee will develop a report about what can be concluded from these studies and also draw conclusions about the potential for future work to improve upon the quality of existing evidence.

Issues and questions to be examined include the following:

1. Does the available evidence provide a reasonable basis for drawing conclusions about the magnitude of capital punishment's effect on homicide rates?
2. Are there differences among the extant analyses that provide a basis for resolving the differences in findings? Are the differences in findings due to inherent limitations in the data? Are there existing statistical methods and/or theoretical perspectives that have yet to be applied that can better address the deterrence question? Are the limitations of existing evidence reflective of a lack of information about the social, economic, and political underpinnings of homicide rates and/or the administration of capital punishment that first must be resolved before the deterrent effect of capital punishment can be determined?
3. Do potential remedies to shortcomings in the evidence on the deterrent effect of capital punishment have broader applicability for research on the deterrent effect of noncapital sanctions?

In addressing those questions, we focused on the studies that have been undertaken since the earlier assessment (National Research Council, 1978). That assessment has stood largely unchallenged: none of the recent work, whatever its conclusion regarding deterrence, relies on the earlier studies criticized in that report or attempts to rehabilitate the value of those studies.

It is important to make clear what is not in the committee's charge. Deterrence is but one of many considerations relevant to deciding whether the death penalty is good public policy. Not all supporters of capital punishment base their argument on deterrent effects, and not all opponents would be affected by persuasive evidence of such effects. The case for capital punishment is sometimes based on normative retributive arguments that the death penalty is the only appropriate and proportional response to especially heinous crimes; the case against it is sometimes based on similarly normative claims that the sanctity of human life precludes state-sanctioned killings, regardless of any possible social benefits of capital punishment. Separate from normative considerations, deterrence is not the only empirical issue relevant to the debate over capital punishment. Other considerations include whether capital punishment can be administered in a nondiscriminatory and consistent fashion, whether the risk of a mistaken execution of an innocent person is acceptably small, and the cost of administering the death penalty in comparison with other sanction alternatives.

Although there is empirical evidence on the issues of discrimination, mistakes, and cost, the charge to the committee does not include these questions. Nor have we been charged with rendering an overall judgment on whether capital punishment is good public policy. We have been tasked only with assessing the scientific quality of the post-*Gregg* evidence on the deterrent effect of capital punishment and making recommendations for improving the scientific quality and policy relevance of future research.

In including recommendations for future research, the study's statement of task recognized that potential remedies to shortcomings in the evidence on the deterrent effect of capital punishment on homicide might also be used in the study of the crime prevention effects of noncapital sanctions. Thus, this report also offers recommendations for improving the scientific quality and policy relevance of that research.

The post-*Gregg* studies can be divided into two types on the basis of the type of data analyzed. *Panel data studies* analyze sets of states or counties measured over time, usually from about 1970 to 2000. These studies relate homicide rates over time and the jurisdictions covered to the legal status of capital punishment or the frequency of executions or both. Time-series studies generally cover only a single geographic unit, which may be as large as a nation or as small as a city. These studies usually examine whether there are short-term changes in homicide rates in that geographic unit in the aftermath of an execution. We review and critique these two types of studies separately because their design and statistical methods are quite different.

Assessing the deterrent effect of the death penalty is much more than a question of interest to social science research. It is a matter of importance to U.S. society at large, and we expect that a potentially broad audience will want to understand how the committee reached its conclusions. Yet the research that the committee has had to appraise is a body of formal empirical work that makes use of highly technical concepts and techniques. The committee has been mindful of the importance of reaching as broad an audience as possible while meeting the fundamental requirement that the report be scientifically grounded. With this in mind, Chapters 1, 2, and 3 (as well as the summary) have been written for a broad, largely policy audience, largely avoiding technical language. In contrast, Chapters 4 and

5 include some exposition and analyses that are aimed for the researchers in the field.

Chapter 2 summarizes homicide rates and the legal status and practice of execution in the United States from 1950 to the present. Chapter 3 provides an overview of the possible mechanisms by which the legal status and practice of execution might affect homicide rates and also provides a nontechnical primer on some of the key challenges to making valid inferences about the deterrent effect of the death penalty. Chapters 4 and 5 review and assess the panel and time-series studies, respectively. Chapter 6 elaborates on the theoretical and statistical challenges to drawing valid conclusions about the deterrent effect of the death penalty, and presents our conclusions and recommendations for future research.

REFERENCES

Berk, R. (2005). New claims about executions and general deterrence: Déjà vu all over again? *Journal of Empirical Legal Studies, 2*(2), 303-330.

Cochran, J.K., and Chamlin, M.B. (2000). Deterrence and brutalization: The dual effects of executions. *Justice Quarterly, 17*(4), 685-706.

Dezhbakhsh, H., Rubin, P.H., and Shepherd, J.M. (2003). Does capital punishment have a deterrent effect? New evidence from postmoratorium panel data. *American Law and Economics Review, 5*(2), 344-376.

Donohue, J.J., and Wolfers, J. (2005). Uses and abuses of empirical evidence in the death penalty debate. *Stanford Law Review, 58*(3), 791-845.

Donohue, J.J., and Wolfers, J. (2009). Estimating the impact of the death penalty on murder. American *Law and Economics Review, 11*(2), 249-309.

Kovandzic, T.V., Vieraitis, L.M., and Boots, D.P. (2009). Does the death penalty save lives? *Criminology & Public Policy, 8*(4), 803-843.

Mocan, H.N., and Gittings, R.K. (2003). Getting off death row: Commuted sentences and the deterrent effect of capital punishment. *Journal of Law & Economics, 46*(2), 453-478.

National Research Council. (1978). *Deterrence and Incapacitation: Estimating the Effects of Criminal Sanctions on Crime Rates.* Panel on Research on Deterrent and Incapacitative Effects, A. Blumstein, J. Cohen, and D. Nagin (Eds.). Committee on Research on Law Enforcement and Criminal Justice. Assembly of Behavioral and Social Sciences. Washington, DC: National Academy Press.

Rubin, P.H. (2009). Don't scrap the death penalty. *Criminology & Public Policy, 8*(4), 853-859.

Shepherd, J.M. (2004). *Testimony on Crime and Deterrence: Hearing on H.R. 2934, the Terrorist Penalties Enhancement Act of 2003.* Subcommittee on Crime, Terrorism, and Homeland Security, House Judiciary Committee. Available: http://judiciary.house.gov/legacy/shepherd042104.pdf [January 2012].

Shepherd, J.M. (2005). Deterrence versus brutalization: Capital punishment's differing impacts among states. *Michigan Law Review, 104*(2), 203-255.

Thomson, E. (1999). Effects of an execution on homicides in California. *Homicide Studies, 3*(2), 129-150.

Zimmerman, P.R. (2009). Statistical variability and the deterrent effect of the death penalty. *American Law and Economics Review, 11*(2), 370-398.

2

Capital Punishment in
the Post-*Gregg* Era

The resurgence in the use of the death penalty in the aftermath of *Gregg*, which followed the de facto moratorium of the 1960s and early 1970s, created the empirical basis for the post-*Gregg* capital punishment deterrence studies. This chapter provides an empirical summary of the legal status and use of capital punishment during this period.

EXECUTIONS AND DEATH SENTENCES OVER TIME

Figure 2-1 shows executions in the United States from 1930 through 2010. As can be seen, executions were more common prior to World War II than in the postwar era. Executions peaked at 199 in 1935. Following the war, executions steadily declined, from 153 in 1947 to 0 in the late 1960s. From 1967 to the *Furman* decision in 1972, there were no executions even though they were legally permissible. (The *Furman* rendered executions legally impossible from 1972 through 1976.) Following the *Gregg* decision in 1976, the number of executions rose rather steadily to the 1999 peak of 98. It then began falling again: by 2005, the number of executions had nearly halved to 53. Since 2005 the number of executions has remained stable at about 50 per year. From 1976 to 2010, a total of 1,234 people were executed.

Also relevant to the evidence on deterrence is the number of death sentences imposed: Figure 2-2 shows the number of those sentences, as well as the number of executions, for the post-*Gregg* period. In 1977, the first full year following the *Gregg* decision, 137 death sentences were imposed. Thereafter, death sentences rose to an annual peak of about 300 in the late

15

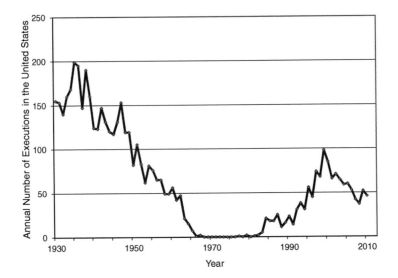

FIGURE 2-1 Annual number of executions in the United States from 1930 to 2010.
SOURCE: Bureau of Justice Statistics (2010, Figure 2).

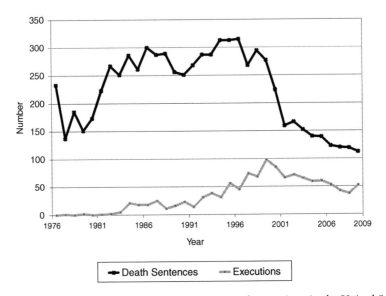

FIGURE 2-2 Annual number of death sentences and executions in the United States from 1976 to 2009.
SOURCE: Bureau of Justice Statistics (2010, Tables 13, 19).

1990s. Since then there has been a steady decline, to 112 in 2009. Figure 2-2 makes clear that far more death sentences are imposed than are carried out.

When a defendant is convicted and sentenced to death, theoretically what follows is an execution. An execution, however, does not follow a death sentence very swiftly or at all for a variety of reasons. The Bureau of Justice Statistics reports that only 15 percent of people sentenced to death between 1973 and 2009 had been executed by the end of 2009. Of these cases, 46 percent ended in alternate ways, including reversed convictions, commuted sentences, or the death of the inmate. Thus, 39 percent of the inmates sentenced to death during the 36-year period were still on death row in December 2009. These inmates, on average, had been under a death sentence for more than 12 years. Because of the smaller number of executions than death sentences every year, the death row population has increased steadily over this period. The number of prisoners facing a death sentence was a little over 400 in 1977 (the first full year after reinstatement); by 2009 it was close to 3,200 (Bureau of Justice Statistics, 2010, Table 18).

These national-level data conceal large differences across states in the use of the death penalty. During the post-*Gregg* era, the death penalty was not legal in all states, and in some states it was only legal for part of the period. Also, among states authorizing the death penalty, in at least some cases there were very large differences in the *extent* of the legal authority for capital punishment and the frequency with which that authority was used. Notably, these variations across states and over time in the legal authority to impose the death penalty and the frequency with which that authority was exercised created the empirical basis for the deterrence studies reviewed in this report.

Table 2-1 shows the legal authority for a death sentence by state from 1976 to 2009. A geographically and otherwise diverse group of 10 states never authorized the use of the death penalty during this period: Alaska, Hawaii, Iowa, Maine, Michigan, Minnesota, North Dakota, Vermont, Wisconsin, and West Virginia. Of the other 40 states, 29 provided that authority for the whole period. The remaining 11 states experienced changes in death penalty authority from 1976 to 2009:

- Two states—North Carolina and Wyoming—transitioned in 1977, immediately after the *Gregg* decision.
- Four states—Kansas, New Hampshire, Oregon, and South Dakota—transitioned from non–death penalty to death penalty status after 1977.
- Two states—New Mexico and Rhode Island—transitioned from death penalty to non–death penalty status after 1977.

TABLE 2-1 Legal Status of Execution in the Post-*Gregg* Era

State	Legal Authority for Death Penalty 1976-2009
Alabama	Yes
Alaska	No
Arizona	Yes
Arkansas	Yes
California	Yes
Colorado	Yes
Connecticut	Yes
Delaware	Yes
Florida	Yes
Georgia	Yes
Hawaii	No
Idaho	Yes
Illinois	Yes
Indiana	Yes
Iowa	No
Kansas	No, 1976-1992; Yes, 1993-2009
Kentucky	Yes
Louisiana	Yes
Maine	No
Maryland	Yes
Massachusetts	No, 1977-1979; Yes, 1980-1983; No, 1984-2009
Michigan	No
Minnesota	No
Mississippi	Yes
Missouri	Yes
Montana	Yes
Nebraska	Yes
Nevada	Yes
New Hampshire	No, 1976-1989; Yes, 1990-2009
New Jersey	No, 1976-1981; Yes, 1982-2005; No, 2006-2009
New Mexico	Yes, 1976-2007; No, 2008-2009
New York	No, 1976-1994; Yes, 1995-2006; No, 2007-2009
North Carolina	No, 1976; Yes, 1977-2009
North Dakota	No
Ohio	Yes
Oklahoma	Yes
Oregon	No, 1976-1977; Yes, 1978-2009
Pennsylvania	Yes
Rhode Island	Yes, 1976-1983; No, 1984-2009
South Carolina	Yes

TABLE 2-1 Continued

State	Legal Authority for Death Penalty 1976-2009
South Dakota	No, 1976-1978; Yes, 1979-2009
Tennessee	Yes
Texas	Yes
Utah	Yes
Vermont	No
Virginia	Yes
Washington	Yes
West Virginia	No
Wisconsin	No
Wyoming	No, 1976; Yes, 1977-2009

SOURCES: Data from Bureau of Justice Statistics (2010), Rogers (2002), and Death Penalty Information Center (2010b).

- Three states—Massachusetts, New Jersey, and New York—transitioned from a non–death penalty to a death penalty status and back to a non–death penalty status over the period.

Thus, from 1976 to 2009 there were 14 transitions in death penalty status among the 50 states. This fact has important implications for estimating the deterrent effect of providing the legal authority for the death penalty independent of the frequency of its use. This issue is discussed at length in Chapter 5.

There is considerable variation among states that authorize the death penalty regarding the types of cases in which death is an allowable punishment. While deterrence studies often focus on homicide rates, there are no states in which the death penalty is available for all intentional homicides. First, not all intentional homicides are murders: many prosecutions that begin as homicide cases are mitigated to the lesser crime of manslaughter, for which capital punishment is never available. Second, even in most states that authorize the death penalty, capital punishment is only available for the relatively narrow category of "first-degree" murders, typically those committed with "premeditation" or those committed during the course of serious felonies. Finally, even those guilty of first-degree murder can only be sentenced to death if the jury finds one or more specified aggravating circumstances. These specified circumstances vary somewhat from state to state, but typically include such factors as the murder of a police officer or witness, murder for hire, murder by a sentenced prisoner, multiple murders or killings that caused a serious risk of death to many people, and murders that are especially "heinous, atrocious, or cruel," which is generally interpreted to mean killings that inflicted torture or extreme degrees of physical or psychological pain on the victim beyond that inherent in the act of killing.

The research reviewed in this report is not always clear in its use of such terms as "homicide" and "murder." Homicide is a generic term meaning the killing of one human being by another (as distinct from suicide or accidental death). Some homicides (e.g., killings in legitimate self-defense or executions pursuant to judicial judgment) are not criminal at all. Criminal homicides are subdivided into various categories of crime (e.g., murder, manslaughter, negligent homicide), depending on whether the person causing death intended to do so or was merely reckless or negligent and on other circumstances surrounding the killing, and these categories are often further subdivided into degrees (e.g., murder in the first degree). Capital punishment is typically only available for the most serious instances of murder.

Most of the studies we reviewed examine the association between capital punishment and the combined number or rate of all types of non-negligent homicides. Unless the specific context dictates otherwise, we use the term "homicide" in describing the findings from the research. When discussing the effect of capital punishment in a broader or more conceptual sense, we use the term "murder," since the conduct that the death penalty typically aims to deter is unjustified intentional killing, which often (but not always) falls into that legal category.

We recognize that neither of these usages is entirely precise as a reflection of legal categories, but the legal complexity (and diversity across the states) of the legal categories, and the general tendency of the social science literature to ignore these distinctions altogether, leave us with no entirely satisfactory alternative.

USE OF THE DEATH PENALTY

As we discuss in Chapter 3, there are no data on the fraction of murders that are eligible for capital punishment, and studies of this issue have reached varying conclusions. One nationwide study (Fagan, Zimring, and Geller, 2006) concluded that about 25 percent of homicides are capital eligible; in contrast, a Missouri study estimated that more than 70 percent of all intentional homicides were at least theoretically capital eligible (Barnes, Sloss, and Thaman, 2009). However, these kinds of studies are inherently problematic. In the absence of an authoritative adjudication, the "facts" of any given homicide can only be gleaned from police reports and other accounts that do not necessarily reliably describe the facts that could be proven sufficiently in a court of law to support a finding of capital eligibility.

Whatever the percentage of homicides that could hypothetically be charged as capital, the percentage that *are* so charged, even at a very early stage of the criminal process, is much smaller, and the number in which a capital verdict is handed down, or a defendant actually executed, is minute in comparison to the homicide rate. Cook (2009) reports that in North Carolina for the fiscal years 2005 and 2006, 26.5 percent of murder arraignments (N = 1,034) were initially charged as capital offenses, and of those that were capitally prosecuted 4 percent were ultimately sentenced to death.

The Cook study also illustrates that, even if a case is initially treated by prosecutors as capital eligible, it is very unlikely to result in a death sentence. There were many reasons for the precipitous drop-off in capital cases between arraignment and sentencing. A small fraction of cases were dismissed or found not guilty at trial. More commonly, defendants pleaded guilty and received a noncapital sentence in return for the plea. In jury trials, some individuals were found guilty of manslaughter or second-, not first-, degree murder, and among those found guilty of first-degree murder most juries did not recommend the death penalty.

Table 2-2 shows summary statistics on the frequency of executions and death sentences from 1973 to 2009 for the 40 states with active death penalty laws during at least part of the period. We focus on this time period because it is the one used in most panel studies of deterrence. The table shows that executions were very concentrated in a few states. Texas accounted for 37.6 percent of executions from 1973 to 2009; Florida, Texas, and Virginia together accounted for 52.2 percent. This concentration is only partly attributable to more frequent imposition of the death penalty by the courts in those states. Other large states, such as California and Pennsylvania, impose relatively large numbers of death sentences. However, the rate at which death sentences are actually carried out varies greatly across states. The last column in Table 2-2 is the ratio of total executions to total death sentences. In California and Pennsylvania, it is only 1.4 percent and 0.8 percent, respectively, compared with 7.0 percent in Florida, 43.0 percent in Texas, and 70.0 percent in Virginia.

Table 2-2 makes clear that in many states death sentences will either never be carried out or will only be carried out after a very long delay. This fact is important for considering the deterrent effect of the death penalty because the longer the delay the more the death penalty resembles a sentence of life without parole, the next most severe sanction to execution. It also complicates the assessment of what features of a capital punishment regime should be tested for an effect on homicide rates: the legal status of capital punishment as a potential sanction, the rate of capital sentences, the rate of executions, or the time to execution. We return to this point in Chapter 3.

Table 2-3 provides perspective on the frequency of executions and

TABLE 2-2 Number of Death Sentences and Executions by Jurisdiction, 1973-2009

	Death Sentences	Executions	Executions per Death Sentence
Federal	65	3	0.0462
Alabama	412	44	0.1068
Arizona	286	23	0.0804
Arkansas	110	27	0.2455
California	927	13	0.0140
Colorado	21	1	0.0476
Connecticut	13	1	0.0769
Delaware	56	14	0.2500
Florida	977	68	0.0696
Georgia	320	46	0.1438
Idaho	42	1	0.0238
Illinois	307	12	0.0391
Indiana	100	20	0.2000
Kansas	12	0	0
Kentucky	81	3	0.0370
Louisiana	238	27	0.1134
Maryland	53	5	0.0943
Massachusetts	4	0	0
Mississippi	190	10	0.0526
Missouri	182	67	0.3681
Montana	15	3	0.2000
Nebraska	32	3	0.0938
Nevada	147	12	0.0816
New Hampshire	1	0	0
New Jersey	52	0	0
New Mexico	28	1	0.0357
New York	10	0	0
North Carolina	528	43	0.0814
Ohio	401	33	0.0823
Oklahoma	350	91	0.2600
Oregon	58	2	0.0345
Pennsylvania	399	3	0.0075
Rhode Island	2	0	0
South Carolina	203	42	0.2069
South Dakota	5	1	0.2000
Tennessee	221	6	0.0271
Texas	1,040	447	0.4298
Utah	27	6	0.2222
Virginia	150	105	0.7000
Washington	38	4	0.1053
Wyoming	12	1	0.0833
TOTAL	8,115	1,188	

SOURCE: Bureau of Justice Statistics (2010, Table 20).

death sentences relative to the frequency of homicides in the states that provided the authority for capital punishment for all or part of the period from 1990 to 1999, the post-*Gregg* decade in which the most executions occurred. The final two columns in the table report the ratios of total death sentences and total executions, respectively, to the total homicides for the period. The statistics make clear that relative to total homicides, death sentences are rare and executions ever rarer. Among states with more than 500 homicides, Oklahoma had the highest ratio of death sentences to homicides, 4.9 percent. Those ratios for Texas and Virginia, the two states that most frequently impose the death penalty were 2.1 percent and 1.4 percent, respectively. The ratio of executions to homicides was even smaller. Among states with more than 500 homicides, the rate never exceeds 1 percent except in Virginia.

The data in Table 2-3 highlight two important challenges to inferring the deterrent effect of the death penalty. Because the fraction of murders resulting in a death sentence is small and the fraction that results in executions even smaller, absolute differences in these fractions between the high and low use states are correspondingly small. It is these small absolute differences that typically form the basis for statistical inferences about the deterrent effect of the death penalty in the panel-type studies. The second problem results from the relative infrequency of homicide in small states. Eight states in Table 2-3 averaged fewer than 50 homicides per year for the 1990-1999 period. Overall, in absolute terms, the numbers of death sentences and executions has been very small. It is these rare events that are the basis for trying to determine what would-be murderers calculate to infer the risk of execution.

The infrequency of executions has been interpreted to mean that there is insufficient variation in the data to detect the effect of capital punishment (see, e.g., Donohue and Wolfers, 2005, p. 794). However, the problem is not that a deterrent effect cannot be estimated from the data: as shown in Table 4-1, there is no shortage of statistically significant results that are reported. Rather, the problem is that the inferences drawn from those data on the impact of the death penalty rest heavily on unsupported assumptions. Although many methodological approaches have been used in the research and analyses, the challenge is to identify credible and informative assumptions that can be combined with the data to draw valid inferences on the deterrent effect of capital sanctions. These issues are discussed further in Chapter 4 on panel studies.

TABLE 2-3 Death Sentences, Executions, and Homicides by State: 1990-1999

Jurisdiction	Death Sentences	Executions	Homicides	Death Sentences per Homicide	Executions per Homicide
Alabama[a]	155	12	3,608	0.0430	0.0033
Arizona	85	19	3,319	0.0256	0.0057
Arkansas	51	21	2,136	0.0239	0.0098
California	334	7	28,781	0.0116	0.0002
Colorado	4	1	1,741	0.0023	0.0006
Connecticut	5	0	1,448	0.0035	0
Delaware	21	10	260	0.0808	0.0385
Florida[b]	185	22	5,711	0.0324	0.0039
Georgia	88	8	6,159	0.0143	0.0013
Idaho	11	1	319	0.0345	0.0031
Illinois	113	12	10,775	0.0105	0.0011
Indiana	26	5	3,931	0.0066	0.0013
Kansas[c]	0	0	304	0	0
Kentucky	25	2	2,134	0.0117	0.0009
Louisiana	79	6	6,409	0.0123	0.0009
Maryland	18	3	5,040	0.0036	0.0006
Mississippi	67	0	2,953	0.0227	0
Missouri	83	39	4,320	0.0192	0.009
Montana[d]	2	2	162	0.0123	0.0123
Nebraska	5	3	491	0.0102	0.0061

State					
New Hampshire[e]	0	0	174	0	0
New Jersey	20	0	3,313	0.006	0
New Mexico	5	0	1,450	0.0034	0
New York	5	0	15,227	0.0003	0
North Carolina	237	11	6,123	0.0387	0.0018
Ohio	127	1	5,337	0.0238	0.0002
Oklahoma	109	19	2,226	0.049	0.0085
Oregon	32	2	1,129	0.0283	0.0018
Pennsylvania	151	3	6,410	0.0236	0.0005
South Carolina	63	21	3,007	0.021	0.007
South Dakota	4	0	110	0.0364	0
Tennessee	57	0	4,492	0.0127	0
Texas	343	162	16,120	0.0213	0.01
Utah	5	3	518	0.0097	0.0058
Virginia	62	63	4,562	0.0136	0.0138
Washington	18	3	2,203	0.0082	0.0014
Wyoming	1	1	141	0.0071	0.0071

NOTE: Table includes only states with the legal authority for use of the death penalty for some part of this period.

[a]Alabama data include only 1990-1998 because homicide rates were not available for 1999.

[b]Florida data include only 1990 and 1992-1996 because homicide rates were not available for 1991 and 1997-1999.

[c]Kansas data include only 1991-1992 because homicide rates were not available for 1993-1999.

[d]Montana data include only 1991, 1992, and 1995 because homicide rates were not available for 1993 and 1994.

[e]New Hampshire data include only 1990-1996 and 1998-1999 because homicide rates were not available for 1997.

SOURCES: Data on executions from Espy and Smykla (2004), data on death sentences from Death Penalty Information Center (2010a), data on homicides from Bureau of Justice Statistics (2009).

REFERENCES

Barnes, K., Sloss, D., and Thaman, S. (2009). Place matters (most): An empirical study of prosecutorial decision-making in death-eligible cases. *Arizona Law Review, 51*(2), 305-379.

Bureau of Justice Statistics. (2009). *Homicide—State Level Trends in One Variable.* Available:
http://bjs.ojp.usdoj.gov/dataonline/Search/Homicide/State/TrendsinOneVar.cfm [January
2011].

Bureau of Justice Statistics. (2010). *Capital Punishment, 2009—Statistical Tables.* U.S. Department of Justice. Available: http://bjs.ojp.usdoj.gov/index.cfm?ty=pbdetail&iid=2215
[December 2011].

Cook, P.J. (2009). Potential savings from abolition of the death penalty in North Carolina.
American Law and Economics Review, 11(2), 498-529.

Death Penalty Information Center. (2010a). *Death Sentences in the United States from 1977
by State and by Year.* Available: http://www.deathpenaltyinfo.org/death-sentences-united-
states-1977-2008 [September 2011].

Death Penalty Information Center. (2010b). *State by State Database.* Available: http://www.
deathpenaltyinfo.org/state_by_state [January 2011].

Donohue, J.J., and Wolfers, J. (2005). Uses and abuses of empirical evidence in the death
penalty debate. *Stanford Law Review, 58*(3), 791-845.

Espy, M.W., and Smykla, J.O. (2004). *Executions in the United States, 1608-2002: The Espy
File.* Available: http://www.deathpenaltyinfo.org/executions-us-1608-2002-espy-file [De-
cember 2011].

Fagan, J., Zimring, F.E., and Geller, A. (2006). Capital punishment and capital murder:
Market share and the deterrent effects of the death penalty. *Texas Law Review, 84*(7),
1803-1867.

Rogers, A. (2002). "Success-at long last": The abolition of the death penalty in Massachusetts,
1928-1984. *Boston College Third World Law Journal, 22*(2), 281-354.

3

Determining the Deterrent Effect of Capital Punishment: Key Issues

Many people have strongly held views on the deterrent effect of the death penalty. To some a deterrent effect is self-evident—who would not at least take pause before committing murder when the potential consequence may be forfeiting one's own life? To others it is equally self-evident that there is no deterrent effect due to the rarity of the imposition of the death penalty and the emotionally charged circumstances of most murders. Both views may have some merit, as the deterrent effect of the death penalty may vary across persons and circumstances. This chapter provides an overview of the difficulties of empirical analysis of the potential deterrent effect. The difficulties arise both from conceptual issues about how the death penalty might deter and from statistical issues that must be successfully overcome to measure the size of that effect, if any.

To argue for the deterrent effect of the death penalty in such ways as "because the death penalty increases the price of murder, there will be less of it" is to gloss over critical elements of understanding how it might work. The magnitude of the deterrent effect of the death penalty, including the possibility of no effect, will depend both on the scope of the legal authority for its use and on the way that legal authority is actually administered. It might also depend on such factors as the publicity given to executions, which are beyond the direct control of the criminal justice system.

One reflection of this complexity is that research on the deterrent effect of capital punishment in the post-*Gregg* era has itself examined diverse issues. Some studies have attempted to assess whether the legal status of capital punishment is related to the homicide rate. And some of these studies have addressed whether statewide homicide rates are associated with whether capital punishment is a legally permissible sanction. Other studies have examined whether homicide rates are associated with moratoriums on executions ordered by governors or courts. There is also a distinct set of studies that have examined whether the frequency of and publicity given to actual executions are related to homicide rates. One part of this research has examined whether execution events seem to affect homicide rates; another part has examined whether homicide rates are associated with various measures of the probability of being executed for homicide.

Our overview of key challenges to making an empirical assessment of the effect of capital punishment on homicide rates is necessarily selective. There is an enormous research literature on the mechanisms by which legal sanctions, of which the death penalty is but one, might affect crime rates. There is also a very large research literature on the econometric and statistical methods used to estimate the effect of the death penalty on homicide rates. We focus on those issues that are particularly important to the reviews and critiques of the panel and time-series literatures in Chapters 4 and 5, respectively. These issues include data limitations, factors beyond the death penalty that contribute to large differences in murder rates across place and over time, possible feedback effects by which homicide rates might affect the administration of the death penalty, how sanction risks are perceived, and the concept of a sanction regime.

There is also a literature that examines the argument that executions may actually exacerbate homicide rates through a brutalization effect. This argument has been studied using the same statistical tools as deterrence, although the mechanism being studied is different. With one exception, all of these are time-series studies, and we review them in Chapter 5.

CONCEPTS OF DETERRENCE

Going back at least 200 years to the legal philosophers Cesare Beccaria in Italy and Jeremy Bentham in England, scholars have speculated on the deterrent effect of official sanctions. At its most basic level, deterrence is typically understood as operating within a theory of choice in which would-be offenders balance the benefits and costs of crime. In the context of murder, the benefits may be tangible, such as pecuniary gain or silencing a potential witness, but they may also involve intangibles, such as defending one's honor, expressing outrage, demonstrating dominance, or simply seeking thrills. The potential costs of crime are comparably varied. Crime can entail personal risk if the victim resists (see, e.g., Cook, 1986). It may also invoke pangs of conscience or shame (see, e.g., Braithwaite, 1989).

In this report we are mainly concerned with the response of would-be offenders to the sanction costs that may result from the commission of murder. Such sanction costs will typically include lengthy imprisonment. Properly understood, the relevant question regarding the deterrent effect of capital punishment is the *differential* or *marginal* deterrent effect of execution over the deterrent effect of other available or commonly used penalties. We emphasize "differential" because it is important to recognize that the alternative to capital punishment is not no punishment or a minor punishment such as probation. Instead, it is a lengthy prison sentence—often life without the possibility of parole.

The theory of deterrence is predicated on the idea that if state-imposed sanction costs are sufficiently severe, certain, and swift, criminal activity will be discouraged. Concerning the severity dimension, a necessary condition for state-sanctioned executions to deter crime is that, at least for some, capital punishment is deemed an even worse fate than the possibility of a lifetime of imprisonment.[1] Severity alone, however, cannot deter. There must also be some possibility that the sanction will be incurred if the crime is committed. For that to happen, the offender must be apprehended, charged, successfully prosecuted, and sentenced by the judiciary. As discussed in Chapter 2, none of these successive stages in processing through the criminal justice system is certain. Thus, another key concept in deterrence theory is the certainty of punishment. Many of the studies of the deterrent effect of capital punishment attempt to estimate whether homicide rates seem to be affected by variation in various measures of the likelihood of execution beyond the likelihood of apprehension and conviction.

Across the social science disciplines, the concepts of certainty and severity have been made operational in deterrence research in very different ways. In Becker's (1968) seminal economic formulation of criminal decision making, individual perceptions of certainty and severity are assumed to correspond to reality. The decision to commit a crime is also assumed to correspond with a precisely formulated set of axioms that define rational decision making. In contrast, among criminologists, models of criminal decision making are less mathematically formalized and place great emphasis on the role of perceptions. These models also explicitly acknowledge that perceptions of certainty and severity may diverge substantially from reality and are probably heavily influenced by experience with the criminal justice system (Cook, 1980; Nagin, 1998). More recent theorizing about criminal decision making also incorporates insights from behavioral economics on biases in risk perceptions to better model the linkage between sanction risk perceptions and reality (Durlauf and Nagin, 2011; Kleiman, 2009; Pogarsky, 2009). For example, prospect

---

[1]Another way sanctions may prevent crime is by making it physically impossible for the offender to commit another crime. Execution achieves this end by the death of the offender. Note, however, that a death sentence will not, on the margin, be more effective in preventing crime (outside a prison) than the incapacitation that accompanies a sentence of life imprisonment without parole.

theory (Kahneman and Tversky, 1979) predicts that low probability events, such as execution, are either overweighted compared to models based on objective probabilities or not considered at all. While each of these perspectives on the deterrence process shares a common view that criminal decision making involves a balancing of costs and benefits, the conceptualization of how this balancing occurs varies greatly across theories. Most importantly for our purposes, the different models are based on different conceptions of how sanction risks are perceived and affect behavior.

A less studied dimension of the classical formulation of deterrence is the concept of celerity—the speed with which a sanction is imposed. In the case of the death penalty, celerity may be a particularly important dimension of the classical formulation. According to the Bureau of Justice Statistics (2010), the average time to execution for the executions that occurred between 1984 and 2009 was 10 years. This statistic, however, pertains only to the small minority of persons sentenced to death who have actually been executed. Only 15 percent of death sentences imposed since 1976 have been carried out. Thus, some individuals have been on death row for decades and indeed may die by other causes before they can be executed. Indeed, according to the Bureau of Justice Statistics (2010, Table 11) there have already been 416 such deaths (1973-2009) among death row inmates. For these offenders, their sentence was, in fact, equivalent to a life sentence.

The studies we review do little to reveal the underlying mechanisms that generate the associations that are estimated between the death penalty and the homicide rate. Indeed, it is possible that these associations reflect social processes that are distinct from deterrence in the narrow sense discussed above. For example, Andenæs (1974) and Packer (1968) speculate that independent of the sanctions prescribed in the criminal laws, the laws themselves may reduce the incidence of the prohibited acts by moral education and related social processes. Thus, providing the legal authority for the use of the death penalty for a special class of murders might prevent murders of that type by making clear that these types of murder are deemed particularly heinous. Alternatively, the brutalization hypothesis predicts the opposite effect.

Given these possible and unknown underlying mechanisms, in the remainder of this report we discuss empirical estimates of the effects of the death on the homicide rate, not "deterrent" effects. Even more important than this point of nomenclature are the implications of alternative possible mechanisms for using empirical findings on the death penalty effects to predict effects on the crime rate of alternative sanction regimes. As we discuss below, alternative mechanisms can imply very different inferences and interpretations. We emphasize this point because the issue of mechanisms is one of several reasons that inferences about the causal effect of capital punishment on homicide rates cannot be reduced to a simple statistical exercise:

the validity of the inferences also depend on the validity of the theories used to construct the statistical models that generate the estimated effects.

The mechanism by which capital punishment might affect homicide rates also has implications for the time frame over which the effect operates. The socialization processes about which Andenæs (1974) and Packer (1968) speculate would likely take years or even decades to materialize and if present would probably operate gradually. Gradual change over long time frames, even if cumulatively large, is often extremely difficult to measure convincingly.

Another issue related to time frame, to which we return in the conclusions of this report, is the processes by which perceptions of sanction risk are formed and are influenced by changes in sanction policy. For example, immediately following the *Gregg* decision, 33 states had capital punishment statutes in place (see Chapter 2). Individual states subsequently followed very different paths in the frequency, relative to the murder rate, with which death penalties were imposed and carried out. If would-be murderers are responsive to this relative frequency, it would take time for them to calibrate the intensity in the state in which they reside and to recognize any changes in intensity resulting from policy shifts. Thus, any effect on homicide rates of changes in the frequency of execution may not occur until after some unknown interval.

The remainder of this chapter lays out key challenges to estimating the causal effect of capital punishment on murder rates. Many of these challenges stem from the necessity of using nonexperimental data to estimate this effect. A useful way of conceptualizing these challenges is to note the important differences between data generated from experiments and data generated under nonexperimental conditions. In an experiment, the effectiveness of a treatment is tested by administering the treatment to a randomly selected group of subjects and comparing their outcomes to another group of randomly selected subjects who receive the control treatment. Randomization of treatment status is intended to ensure the equivalence of the treatment and control groups except for treatment status. The purpose of an experiment is to measure the effect of a specified treatment on one or more outcomes relative to an alternative treatment, generally referred to as the control treatment. Experiments are a widely accepted way of scientifically testing for causal effects: there is general agreement that the findings are reflective of causal effects.

For obvious reasons, it is not possible to conduct a randomized capital punishment experiment. Suppose, however, that such an experiment were possible. In such an experiment, three key features would be relevant: (1) specification of what constitutes treatment, (2) randomization of the capital punishment treatment, and (3) experimental control of the treatment. In addition, in an experiment, the experimental and control treatment alternatives must be specified prior to the beginning of the experiment, and treatment status is controlled by the experimenter, not the subjects of the experiment. We develop below the implications of each of the features of experiments for the study of the effect of capital punishment with nonexperimental data.

SANCTION REGIMES

A sanction regime defines the way a jurisdiction administers a sanction. In an experiment, the differences between the sanction regimes in the treatment and control jurisdictions would define what constitutes treatment. In a capital punishment jurisdiction, specification of the sanction regime would require a delineation of the types of crimes and offenders that would be eligible for capital punishment and the rules that would be used to determine whether an eligible offender could be sentenced to death. It would also require a specification of the appeals and pardon processes. In addition, sanctions for individuals not sentenced to death would have to be specified. The sanction regime in a jurisdiction without capital punishment would have to be similarly specified. Such an experiment, therefore, would not test the efficacy of "capital punishment" in the abstract. Instead, it would test a particular capital punishment against a specific alternative regime without capital punishment. Only after specification and assignment of the capital and noncapital sanction regimes could the experiment begin and the data collected.

By contrast, in studies based on nonexperimental data, sanction regimes are not specified and assigned prior to data collection. Instead, the researcher has to make assumptions about the theoretically relevant dimensions of the sanction regimes of the entities administering the punishment, usually states. Thus, a key question in an assessment of the validity of a capital punishment study involves those assumptions: How convincingly does a study specify and explain aspects of the capital punishment sanction regime it is studying?

The legal status of the death penalty in the jurisdiction is one relevant dimension of a sanction regime. States with and without the death penalty have clearly defined differences in their sanction regimes. However, the numerous differences across states in the types of offenses that are capital eligible and the administrative processes related to the imposition and appeal of the death sentences (as described in Chapter 2) may be relevant to defining aspects of the sanction regime that have the potential to influence deterrence. For example, Frakes and Harding (2009) attempt to examine whether the explicit delineation of the killing of a child as an aggravating circumstance for the use of the death penalty deters child murder. Still another important dimension of the sanction regime is the severity of noncapital sanctions for murder in both capital and noncapital punishment states, a point we return to below.

A sanction regime is also defined by how aggressively the authority to use the death penalty is actually applied. Among states that provide authority for the use of the death penalty, the frequency with which that authority is used varies greatly. As pointed out in Chapter 2, since 1976 three states—Florida, Texas, and Virginia—have accounted for more than one-half of all executions carried out in the United States, even though 40 states and the federal government provided the legal authority for the death penalty for at least part of this period. Constructing measures of the intensity with which capital punishment is used in states with that authority is a particularly daunting problem. In an experiment, the intensity of application would have to be specified ex ante by delineating the circumstances in which capital punishment should be applied. With nonexperimental data, intensity must be inferred ex post by the rate of application. The panel studies calculate intensity by an assortment of measures of the probability of execution based on variations over time and among states in the frequency of executions to distinguish, for example, the very different sanction regimes of Texas and California. Chapter 4 discusses these measures at length.

The concept of deterrence predicts that one relevant dimension of a sanction regime is the probability of execution given conviction for a capital eligible murder. However, if deterrence is predicated on the *perception* of the risk of execution, short-term or even longer term variations in the rate of executions may not produce changes in the homicide rate, even if the death penalty is a deterrent. If such temporal variation in the actual rate of administration is perceived as confirming stable perceptions about this probability, rather than signaling change in the probability, such variations will not be associated with changes in the homicide rate even though the intensity of the use of capital punishment does deter.

An example from gambling on the outcome of the role of a dice can illustrate this point. Suppose a person knows that the dice are fair. For that person, the actual outcomes of successive roles of the dice will not cause the person to change the estimate that the chance of each number is 1/6. Therefore, that person's betting patterns will not change in response to short-term variations in the frequency of each of the numbers 1 to 6. The analog for deterrence research is that variations over time in the actual frequency of executions may not alter would-be murderers perceptions of the risk of execution and therefore not alter behavior even if there is a deterrent effect.

However, it is possible that perceptions are influenced by the actual outcomes. If so, a bettor's betting pattern would change in response to the outcomes of the dice rolls. But if this is the case, it is necessary to posit a specific model of how those perceptions change to infer how behavior changes. For example, the so-called gambler's fallacy (Gilovich, 1983) posits that if one number, say 6, is rolled several times in a row, people will surmise that the probability of a 6 is reduced at least temporarily and thus reduce their betting on 6. In the context of deterrence, the gambler's fallacy model suggests that the event of an execution might increase, not decrease, murders because people will surmise that the probability of execution has declined at least temporarily. Alternatively, people may surmise that the dice is weighted to favor 6 and therefore increase their betting on 6. Under this model, the event of an execution might cause individuals to increase their perception of the risk of execution and thereby reduce the murder rate. We do not specifically endorse any of these models of risk perception. Our purpose in this discussion is to emphasize that in the analysis of nonexperimental data, the sanction regime must be constructed ex post on the basis of the researcher's assumptions about theoretically relevant constructs. In turn, this fact implies that the relevant dimensions of a sanction regime cannot be specified outside of a model of sanction risk perceptions and their effect on behavior.

It is a truism that sanction threats cannot deter unless at least some would-be offenders are aware of the threat. There is a large literature on sanction risk perceptions that demonstrates that the general public is very poorly informed about actual sanction levels and the frequency of their imposition (Apel, in press). These studies might be interpreted as demonstrating that legal sanctions cannot deter (since people do not really know what they are). This interpretation neglects the possibility that some would-be offenders may be deterred by the mere knowledge that there is a criminal sanction even if the severity of the sanction is not specifically known to them. Moreover, most people do not commit crimes for a host of reasons that are unrelated to the certainty and severity of criminal sanctions. These people have no reason to know, for example, the frequency with which executions are carried out, because they have no intention of committing murder. Some degree of deterrence only requires that some people who are actively considering committing a crime are aware of the penalties and that their behavior is influenced by this awareness.

Still, as the dice example illustrates, the issue of how the death penalty sanction is perceived is fundamental to the interpretation of the evidence on its deterrent effect. Consider an actual, not hypothetical, example. Donohue and Wolfers (2005) compared trends in homicide rates between states with and without capital punishment from 1960 to 2000, a period that spans the 1972 *Furman* decision that stopped use of the death penalty and 1976 *Gregg* decision that reinstated it. The time-series data for the two states closely track each other, with no obvious perturbations at the time of the *Furman* and *Gregg* decisions. From these data one could conclude there is no obvious evidence that the moratorium on capital punishment or its reinstatement had an effect on murder rates. However, because the last execution prior to the *Furman* decision was in 1967 and executions were rare throughout the 1960s, there are two very different possible interpretations of the data. One interpretation is that the deterrent effect of the potential for a death sentence is small or nonexistent. The other is that the near absence of executions in the decade prior to *Furman* resulted in people's stable perceptions in both abolitionist and nonabolitionist states that there was no realistic chance of the death penalty being imposed. With such perceptions there would be no possibility of a deterrent effect even if would-be murderers would otherwise be deterred by the threat of execution.

The issue of how sanction threats are perceived is also important in correctly interpreting evidence that is taken as reflecting deterrence. For example, some time-series studies report evidence that suggests reduced homicides in the immediate aftermath of an execution. Suppose this is, in fact, a reflection of a causal effect of an execution on murder. Depending on how the threat of execution is perceived, there are a number of very different interpretations of this evidence. One possible model of perceptions is that people respond to the *event* of an execution, with each execution reducing the number of murders that would otherwise occur according to a dose-response relationship relating murders averted to number of executions in a given time frame. A second model is that people respond not to the event of an execution but to the *perceived probability* of execution given commission of a murder, and that the event of an execution causes them to update this perceived probability. In this model, the number of both executions and murders is relevant to the updating process. Unlike the first model, there is no single dose-response relationship between number of executions and murders. If the frequency of execution does not keep pace with the rate of increase in murders, would-be murderers might infer that the probability of execution is declining. Yet a third model of such time-series evidence is that the event of an execution only alters the timing of the murder—a murder averted in the immediate aftermath of an execution occurs at a later date. We do not endorse any of these interpretations: we offer them to make concrete the proposition that the interpretation of evidence requires a model of sanction risk perceptions and of the effect of those perceptions on behavior.[2]

---

[2]We also emphasize that this same observation about the need for a model of sanction risk perceptions and their influence on behavior applies to the interpretation of evidence from an experiment. Only in an impossibly idealized experiment would it be possible to specify the sanction regime in such detail to avoid the need to extrapolate from the experimental findings to explain their implications for unspecified aspects of the sanction regime. Furthermore, even with a completely specified sanction regime, extrapolation of the findings to other settings or modified versions of the tested sanction regime would require a theory of perceptions and behavior.

DATA ISSUES

In any empirical study it is important to question the adequacy of the data used in the analysis. In the context of the studies reviewed for this report a key question is whether the data being used are adequate to produce credible estimates of the effects of those aspects of the sanction regime under investigation.

As noted above, most studies of the deterrent effect of capital punishment are based on U.S. data. Although the U.S. data on murder show far less underreporting than data on other types of crime, the data on murders contain flaws that are important to recognize in studies on deterrence. The murder rates used in most studies include murders that are not eligible for capital punishment, either because of characteristics of the perpetrator (such as age or IQ) or because of characteristics of the offense (such as the absence of legally defined aggravating factors). The supplemental homicide reports, a dataset compiled by the Federal Bureau of Investigation (FBI) that provides more detailed data on homicide incidents than the agency's standardized *Uniform Crime Report*, in principle provide details of the perpetrator and the event that allow researchers to exclude murders that likely are not eligible for capital punishment; but these data have their own set of problems due to widespread recording errors and omissions about characteristics of the perpetrator and the event itself (Messner, Deane, and Beaulieu, 2002; Wadsworth and Roberts, 2008).

As we emphasize above, the deterrent effect of capital punishment is a meaningful concept only relative to another key dimension of the sanction regime—the severity of noncapital sanctions. After all, as a practical question of public policy, the key question is not whether a hypothetical capital punishment regime in which execution is the only available sanction for murder would deter some offenders. Rather, it is whether a plausible capital punishment regime will have a meaningful incremental effect on homicide rates in the United States when added to a specific program of lesser sanctions. Hence, state-level data on alternative punishments are necessary, most specifically, the prison sentence lengths for murders that might also be candidates for capital punishment.

Such data do not exist. This gap is potentially a serious one for studying deterrence. If the severity of noncapital sanctions for murder is correlated with the legal status or the frequency of use of capital punishment, failure to account for the severity of noncapital sanctions may result in serious bias in estimates of deterrent effect. If, for example, capital punishment jurisdictions tended also to impose more severe imprisonment sanctions than noncapital jurisdictions, a reduced level of homicide in such jurisdictions may be attributable to these other features of their sanction regime and not to the death penalty. Or, if capital punishment jurisdictions are otherwise more lenient, any deterrent effect achieved by adding capital punishment might not translate into a similar effect of adding capital punishment in a jurisdiction that already imposes severe prison sentences for murder. Or, if a state relied on the threat of capital punishment to counter an inadequate budget for investigating and prosecuting crimes, the deterrent effect of capital punishment might be masked relative to a noncapital punishment state with more effective crime control policy. Again, we do not endorse any of these hypotheses, but delineate them to illustrate the difficulty of isolating deterrent effects of a single component of any sanction regime.

VARIATIONS IN MURDER RATES

The severity of noncapital sanctions is but one example of other factors that may affect murder rates. If the data being analyzed were the product of a randomized capital punishment experiment, the question of how other factors influence murder rates would not have to be addressed. Randomization of the capital punishment sanction regime would insure that the use of capital punishment was uncorrelated with other factors influencing murder rates. Thus, for example, if a capital punishment sanction regime were randomized across states, capital punishment would not be more commonplace in the Southern states, as in practice it is. By breaking the correlation between treatment, in this case capital punishment, and other factors that may be influencing the outcome of interest, in this case murders, randomization ensures that the capital punishment deterrent effect estimate is not contaminated by the independent influence of these other factors on murder rates. Because capital punishment research is based on nonexperimental data, equivalence of states without and without capital punishment on all other factors is not insured. Hence, consideration of the influence of factors other than capital punishment on murder rates must be addressed.

Homicide rates in the United States vary enormously over time and place. In 2009, Louisiana had the highest statewide rate, 11.8 homicides per 100,000 population; the state with the lowest rate, New Hampshire, had 0.8 homicides per 100,000 population, 93 percent fewer (Bureau of Justice Statistics, 2010; Federal Bureau of Investigation, 2010). Variations over time are also large. Figure 3-1 plots the U.S. homicide rate over the 25-year period from 1974 to 2009. From 1974 to the early 1990s, the rate rose, then fell, then rose again, and then began declining steadily until leveling off in the early 2000s.

As we emphasize throughout this report, these variations are important to making a valid determination of the deterrent effect of the death penalty, because if other influences on the murder rate are correlated with the use of the death penalty, the estimated deterrent effect may be contaminated by the effect of these other influences on the homicide rates. Such other

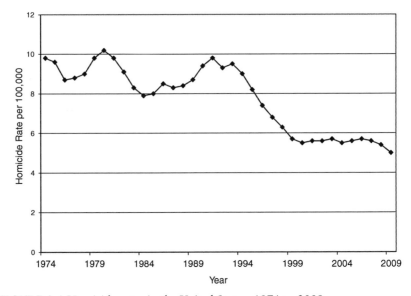

FIGURE 3-1 Homicide rates in the United States: 1974 to 2009.
SOURCES: Data from Bureau of Justice Statistics (2010) and Federal Bureau of Investigation (2010).

influences may reflect factors related to the criminal justice system. One has already been described: the severity of noncapital sanctions. Another is police effectiveness in apprehending murderers. If the probability of apprehension is correlated with the imposition of the death penalty, a finding that the death penalty seemingly deters murders might actually reflect police effectiveness in deterring murder. Such contamination may also come from social, economic, or political factors that affect the homicide rate and that are outside the criminal justice system.

There have been numerous commentaries on the sources of variation in U.S. homicide rates, with many focusing specifically on the sharp drop in homicides since the early 1990s (Blumstein and Wallman, 2000, 2006; Levitt, 2004; Zimring, 2010; Zimring and Fagan, 2000). However, these commentaries provide very limited guidance on how to account for other possible sources of change in homicide rates in a statistical analysis of the deterrent effect of the death penalty.

To provide a concrete illustration of the challenges of inferring the deterrent effects of the death penalty, consider Texas, the state that makes the most frequent use of the death penalty (in absolute numbers). Figure 3-2 plots the annual frequency of executions in Texas from 1974 to 2009. Texas's first post-*Gregg* execution occurred in 1982, and executions re-

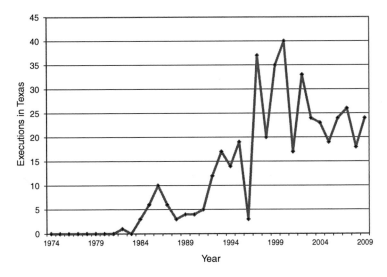

FIGURE 3-2 Executions in Texas: 1974 to 2009.
SOURCES: Data from Espy and Smykla (2004) and Texas Department of Criminal Justice (2011).

mained relatively infrequent until the early 1990s; the frequency then escalated rapidly to a peak of 40 in 2000. Thereafter, there has been drop-off to about 20-25 per year. Figure 3-3 plots the homicide rate in Texas (as well as California and New York) over the same period. The pattern for all three states closely resembles the U.S. national trend. From 1974 through the early 1990s the Texas homicide rate rose then fell and then rose again before falling steadily from 1991 to the early 2000s, when it leveled off. For the period from 1976 to 1991, there is no apparent relationship between the homicide rate and the frequency of execution. However, the steady decline in the homicide rate since 1991 does correspond with the dramatic increase in executions that occurred in the early 1990s. Thus, if the early 1990s is assumed to be the demarcation of Texas shifting to a dramatically higher use of capital punishment, the data are consistent with that shift having a deterrent effect.

However, the data from California and New York challenge that interpretation. The death penalty has been an available sentencing option in California for the entire post-1976 period, but the frequency of executions in California is low in comparison with Texas—from 1976 to 2009, California executed 13 people, and Texas executed 447. Both states, however, *sentenced* sizable numbers of people to death. In this regard, New York offers still another interesting contrast. It sentenced only 10 people to

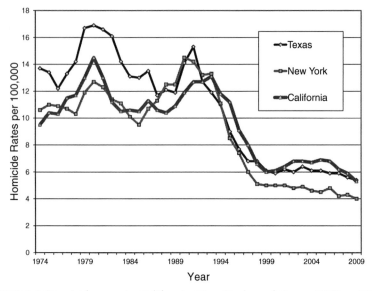

FIGURE 3-3 Homicide rates in California, New York, and Texas: 1974 to 2009.
SOURCES: Data from Bureau of Justice Statistics (2010) and Federal Bureau of
Investigation (2010).

death between 1973 and 2009 and had executed none as of 2009 (Bureau
of Justice Statistics, 2010).[3]

As shown in Figure 3-3, the California, New York, and Texas homicide
rates move in close unison for the entire 1974-2009 period. Like Texas, the
California and New York rates rise, then fall, and then rise between 1974
and the early 1990s; the rates for all three states then begin a steep decline
to the early 2000s and level out. Thus, even though California, New York,
and Texas have made very different use of the death penalty, particularly
since 1990, their homicide rates are remarkably the same over about three
decades.

Our purpose in reporting these data is not to draw any conclusion
about the deterrent effect of the death penalty. The three states were pur-
posely selected to illustrate the importance of accounting for variations,
across time and place, in factors that influence murder rates other than the
use of capital punishment. If informal comparisons of data from a few self-
selected jurisdictions were sufficient to settle the question of the deterrent
effect of the death penalty, the reviews of the panel studies in Chapter 4 and
the of time-series studies in Chapter 5, which are based on application of

---

[3]In New York, the legal authority for the death penalty was available only from 1995 to
2007.

formal statistical methods, would be unnecessary. For example, the panel studies are based on data from all 50 states, not just three selected ones.

In addition, and most critically, any inferences about the effects of the death penalty that are based on the data reported in Figure 3-3 require a conception—that is, a plausible hypothesis—of *how* the death penalty might affect homicide rates. Suppose, as is assumed in some of the time-series studies reviewed in Chapter 5, the residents of these three states respond to deviations away from their state's long-term trend in executions or death sentences and not to the trend lines themselves. Informal inferences based on visual inspection of long-term homicide rates and death penalty sanction trends cannot provide the basis for detecting such relationships: in Chapter 5 we apply the formal statistical methods that can detect those relationship. More generally, if valid inferences about the effect of the death penalty on homicide rates could be drawn from superficial analysis of data plots like those in Figure 3-3, the question of its effect would have been settled long ago. For the committee's discussion of this point, see the section on cross-polity comparisons in Chapter 5.

RECIPROCAL EFFECTS BETWEEN HOMICIDE RATES AND SANCTION REGIMES

In an experiment, one very important consequence of random assignment of treatment is that treatment assignment is not affected by the outcome of interest. For example, in a randomized experiment of the effectiveness of a therapy in reducing depression, the probability of participants receiving the experimental treatment is not influenced by their level of depression at the time of treatment assignment. As a consequence, the direction of causality is clear—any difference in symptoms of depression between the experimental and control groups is a consequence of the treatments assigned and not of the level of depression at the time of treatment. In analyses of nonexperimental data, attribution of direction of causality in an association between two variables is often far less clear.

Going back to deterrence research in the 1960s, there has been concern about the possibility that estimates of deterrent effects were biased by reciprocal effects between crime rates and sanction levels. That is, while sanction levels may be influencing crime rates through the processes of deterrence, crime rates may simultaneously be affecting sanction levels. Crime rates may influence sanctions by a variety of mechanisms. One possibility is that, in the short run, increases in crime may strain the resources committed to the criminal justice system and result in a reduction in overall effective sanction levels. Over the longer term, the political process might respond to rising crime rates by increasing the resources committed to crime control and increasing the severity of sanctions.

The possibility of reciprocal effects greatly complicates estimation of the deterrent effect of capital punishment. For example, suppose that states with high rates of executions (as measured by the percentage of homicides that result in executions) tend also to have lower homicide rates. One interpretation of this negative association is deterrence: that is, more certain application of the death penalty reduces murders. However, if there are reciprocal effects of crime rates on sanction levels, this negative association might just as well reflect the resource saturation effect noted above: that is, higher murder rates and crime rates tend to overwhelm the capacity of the justice system to respond to crime. Higher crimes rates may, for example, reduce the effectiveness of police in apprehending criminals or may make overburdened prosecutors more receptive to accepting plea bargains for noncapital sanctions in order to avoid trials. Both such mechanisms could contribute to reductions in the frequency of executions.

The possibility of reciprocal causation is not addressed in the time-series research, and only a subset of studies in the panel research make any attempt to address this very challenging problem. Given enough assumptions, it is possible to disentangle empirically causal effects in the presence of reciprocal causation. Thus, in principle, in the above example, the deterrent effect of execution certainty can be distinguished from the effect of murder rates on execution certainty. However, such analysis requires the imposition of what are called "identification restrictions." Identification restrictions can come in many forms, and isolating the role of any one restriction is difficult and sometimes impossible.

In the panel studies in which reciprocal causation is addressed, an important component of identification involves the use of "instrumental variables." Chapter 4 includes an extended discussion of the validity of the assumptions that underlie the instrumental variable applications in that research. Here we emphasize only that in the presence of reciprocal causation, estimation of causal effects ultimately depends on more than just the data. This is still another example of the fact that the validity of the estimates of the effects of deterrence depends significantly on modeling assumptions—in this case the plausibility of untestable assumptions about identification restrictions. This is not, by itself, a fatal criticism, since identification restrictions can often be derived from social science theories. However, not all assumptions are equally plausible, so their validity has to be judged in context.

The presence of reciprocal effects also complicates the interpretation of findings on the deterrent effect of the death penalty even if based on plausible identification restrictions. For example, suppose that a state changes its death penalty sanction regime by expanding the types of murders that are eligible for the death penalty and that this change has the desired deterrent effect, which is estimated, based on plausible identification restrictions, to reduce the murder rate by 5 percent. In the presence of feedback effects, the ultimate reduction in the murder rate will not be 5 percent: it may be more or it may be less because the change in the murder rate may affect other aspects of the sanction regime, such as the way prosecutors and defense attorneys approach plea bargains or the resources available to the criminal justice system. These changes, in turn, may further influence the murder rate. Furthermore, the sentencing regime that caused the 5 percent reduction may differ from a regime without the death penalty, not just because of the possibility of a death sentence, but also because the availability of the death penalty as an option provides prosecutors with greater leverage in plea negotiations (which may result in a greater number of long prison sentences) and because the extra resources required to try capital cases may affect the resources available to prosecute and try other crimes.

In North Carolina, for example, 25 percent of first-degree murder cases are initially prosecuted capitally. Each of these cases requires relatively more resources because of extra care for due process. The in-kind costs include the equivalent of nine assistant prosecutors each year, as well as 345 days of trial court time, approximately 10 percent of the resources of the Supreme Court, and $11 million in cash outlays (Cook, 2009). Only after all these feedbacks have played themselves out could the ultimate effect of a change in sanction regime on the murder rate be determined. This kind of feedback is still another reason that throughout this report we describe empirical estimates of the effects of the death penalty as effects on the homicide rate, not as deterrent effects.

SUMMARY

In this and the preceding chapter we lay out some of the key challenges to using data from the studies reviewed in the next two chapters to infer the causal effect of the death penalty on the homicide rate. Some of these challenges can be resolved empirically. For example, with data on the severity of noncapital sanctions, it is possible to test empirically whether the inclusion of these data in the analysis alters estimates of the causal effect of capital punishment on murder rates. More generally, it is also possible to analyze the sensitivity of findings to a specified set of alternative model specifications. We discuss examples of such tests in those chapters.

However, it is also important to recognize that inferences about the effect of alternative capital punishment regimes *cannot* be reduced to purely statistical questions. Interpretations will always depend on assumptions about the underlying mechanisms by which sanction regimes affect behavior and how behavior in turn affects sanction regimes and that those assumptions are not testable with the data used in the analysis. As a consequence, inferences about the effects of capital and noncapital sanction regimes on murder rates will depend on more than the data that generate the estimates: the inferences will also depend on the validity of the theories used to construct the models on which the estimates rest.

REFERENCES

Andenæs, J. (1974). *Punishment and Deterrence.* Ann Arbor: University of Michigan Press.

Apel, R. (in press). Sanctions, perceptions, and crime: Implications for criminal deterrence. Submitted to *Journal of Quantitative Criminology, 28.*

Becker, G.S. (1968). Crime and punishment: An economic approach. *Journal of Political Economy,* 76(2), 169-217.

Blumstein, A., and Wallman, J. (2000). *The Crime Drop in America.* New York: Cambridge University Press.

Blumstein, A., and Wallman, J. (2006). The crime drop and beyond. *Annual Review of Law and Social Science,* 2(1), 125-146.

Braithwaite, J. (1989). *Crime, Shame, and Reintegration.* New York: Cambridge University Press.

Bureau of Justice Statistics. (2010). *Capital Punishment, 2009—Statistical Tables.* Washington, DC: U.S. Department of Justice. Available: http://bjs.ojp.usdoj.gov/index.cfm?ty=pbdetail&iid=2215 [December 2011].

Cook, P.J. (1980). Research in criminal deterrence: Laying the groundwork for the second decade. *Crime and Justice,* 2, 211-268.

Cook, P.J. (1986). The relationship between victim resistance and injury in noncommercial robbery. *Journal of Legal Studies,* 15(2), 405-416.

Cook, P.J. (2009). Potential savings from abolition of the death penalty in North Carolina. *American Law and Economics Review,* 11(2), 498-529.

Donohue, J.J., and Wolfers, J. (2005). Uses and abuses of empirical evidence in the death penalty debate. *Stanford Law Review,* 58(3), 791-845.

Durlauf, S., and Nagin, D. (2011). The deterrent effect of imprisonment. In P.J. Cook, J. Ludwig, and J. McCrary (Eds.), *Controlling Crime: Strategies and Tradeoffs* (pp. 43-94). Chicago: University of Chicago Press.

Espy, M.W., and Smykla, J.O. (2004). *Executions in the United States, 1608-2002: The Espy File.* Available: http://www.deathpenaltyinfo.org/executions-us-1608-2002-espy-file [December 2011].

Federal Bureau of Investigation. (2010). *Crime in the United States 2009.* Washington, DC: Author.

Frakes, M., and Harding, M.C. (2009). The deterrent effect of death penalty eligibility: Evidence from the adoption of child murder eligibility factors. *American Law and Economics Review,* 11(2), 451-497.

Gilovich, T. (1983). Biased evaluation and persistence in gambling. *Journal of Personality and Social Psychology,* 44(6), 1,110-1,126.

Kahneman, D., and Tversky, A. (1979). Prospect theory: An analysis of decision under risk. *Econometrica,* 47(2), 263-291.

Kleiman, M. (2009). *When Brute Force Fails: How to Have Less Crime and Less Punishment.* Princeton, NJ: Princeton University Press.

Levitt, S.D. (2004). Understanding why crime fell in the 1990s: Four factors that explain the decline and six that do not. *The Journal of Economic Perspectives,* 18(1), 163-190.

Messner, S.F., Deane, G., and Beaulieu, M. (2002). A log-multiplicative association model for allocating homicides with unknown victim-offender relationships. *Criminology,* 40(2), 457-480.

Nagin, D.S. (1998). Criminal deterrence research at the outset of the twenty-first century. *Crime and Justice, 23*, 1-42.

Packer, H.L. (1968). *The Limits of the Criminal Sanction*. Stanford, CA: Stanford University Press.

Pogarsky, G. (2009). Deterrence and decision-making: Research questions and theoretical refinements. In M.D. Krohn, A. Lizotte and H.G. Penlly (Eds.), *Handbook on Crime and Deviance* (pp. 241-258). New York: Springer.

Texas Department of Criminal Justice. (2011). *Executed Offenders*. Available: http://www.tdcj.state.tx.us/death_row/dr_executed_offenders.html.

Wadsworth, T.I.M., and Roberts, J.M. (2008). When missing data are not missing: A new approach to evaluating supplemental homicide report imputation strategies. *Criminology, 46*(4), 841-870.

Zimring, F.E. (2010). The scale of imprisonment in the United States: Twentieth century patterns and twenty-first century prospects. *Journal of Criminal Law and Criminology, 100*(3), 1,225-1,246.

Zimring, F.E., and Fagan, J. (2000). The search for causes in an era of crime declines: Some lessons from the study of New York City homicide. *Crime & Delinquency, 46*(4), 446-456.

4

Panel Studies

In this chapter, we discuss the recent research that used panel data and methods to examine whether the death penalty has a deterrent effect on homicide and if so, the size of this effect. As noted in Chapter 1, "panel data" and "panel methods" refer to data from many geographic locations followed over time—usually annual state-level data—and a particular set of multiple regression methods. The annual state data include all states, and the time periods covered are typically from the late 1970s (post-*Gregg*) through the late 1990s or into the 2000s. Over this time period, there have been variations in the frequency of death penalty sentences, executions, and the legal availability of the death penalty. With these types of data, the strategy for identifying an effect of the death penalty on homicides has been, roughly speaking, to compare the variation over time in the average homicide rates among states that changed their death penalty sanctions versus those that did not.

This chapter assesses the extent to which the research using panel data is informative on the question of whether and how much the death penalty has a deterrent effect on homicide. For this assessment, we compare the data and methods used in this literature with those that would be available from an ideal randomized experiment (see Chapter 3). The purpose of this exercise is to clarify the challenges that face researchers using panel methods to study the death penalty and deterrence. We then assess the extent to which this research overcomes these challenges.

This literature is striking in the *similarity* of the data and methods used across studies and the *diversity* of the results. Given this diversity of results across and in some cases within studies, a central task for this committee is to assess the validity of the models used in the studies.

We begin the chapter by describing the key features of the studies we reviewed and giving a brief overview of their data and methods. We then discuss the primary challenges to researchers using panel data and methods to inform the question of whether the death penalty affects the homicide rate: the difficulty in measuring changes over time in the relevant sanction policies for homicide and the difficulties in establishing that any changes in homicides that are concurrent with changes in the death penalty are *caused by* those changes in the death penalty and not vice versa or by other factors that affect both—such as other sanctions for murder. We conclude with our assessment of the informativeness of the panel research.

PANEL STUDIES REVIEWED

Methods Used: Overview

We begin our review of the panel research by briefly describing the regression models used in the studies. Our intention with this description is to establish the extent to which the methods are largely consistent across studies, as context for understanding the particular dimensions on which the studies differ.

The panel research makes use of multiple regression models involving "fixed effects" that take the following form:

$$y_{it} = \alpha_i + \beta_{it} + \gamma f(Z_{it}) + \delta X_{it} + \varepsilon_{it}, \tag{4-1}$$

where y_{it} is the number of homicides per 100,000 residents in state i in year t, $f(Z_{it})$ is an expected cost function of committing a capital homicide that depends on the vector of death penalty or other sanction variables Z_{it} with corresponding parameter γ measuring the effect of the death penalty on the homicide rate. Importantly, this effect is assumed to be homogeneous across states i and years t.

A primary benefit of panel data is that one observes homicide and execution rates in the 50 states over many years. This allows researchers to effectively account for unobserved features of the state or of the time period that might be associated with both the application of the death penalty and the homicide rate. Some states, for example, might have unobserved social norms that lead to higher (or lower) execution rates and lower (or higher) rates or homicide: Texas is arguably different than Massachusetts in this regard. The panel data model in Equation (4-1) accounts for some of these differences with a state-specific intercept parameter, α_i, referred to as a *state fixed effect,* that allows the mean homicide rate to vary additively by state, and a time-specific intercept, β_{it}, referred to as a *time fixed effect*, that allows the mean homicide rate to vary additively over time. These fixed effects account for unobserved factors that are state specific but fixed across time, such as the social norms that make Texas different than Massachusetts, and factors that are year specific but apply to all states, such as macroeconomic events that may affect homicide rates across the country. In addition to these fixed effects, some of the researchers also include state-specific linear time trends that allow each state's homicide rate trend to vary (linearly) from the year-to-year national fluctuations.

The literature also includes a set of covariates, X_{it}, that are intended to control for additional factors that may vary with both state and year. These sets of covariates are largely similar across studies and include economic indicators, such as the unemployment rate and real per capita income; demographic variables, such as the proportion of the state's population in each of several age groups; the proportion of the state's population that is black; and the proportion of the state's population that reside in urban areas. The covariates also include health and policy variables, such as the infant mortality rate, the legal drinking age, and the governor's party affiliation; and crime, policing, or sanctioning variables, such as the number of prisoners per violent crime.

Finally, ε_{it} is a random variable that accounts for the unobserved factors determining the homicide rate.[1] Researchers make two general assumptions about the relationship between the death penalty variables, Z_{it}, and ε_{it}. The most common assumption is that the death penalty, as measured by the variable Z_{it}, is statistically independent of the unobserved factors that determine homicide, as it would be in an ideal randomized experiment. An alternative route is to assume that there is some covariate, termed an *instrumental variable*, that is independent of ε_{it} but not of the death penalty.

The Studies, Their Characteristics, and the Effects Found

Table 4-1 lists the studies reviewed in this chapter and a few of their key characteristics, and briefly notes each one's results.[2] This list does not

---

[1] In estimating these models, the data are typically weighted by state population.

[2] One characteristic that is not highlighted in Table 4-1 is the choice of outcome variable, y_{it}. All of the studies listed in the table and reviewed in this chapter focused on the overall homicide rate (or the log-rate). However, there are a few studies in the panel data literature that examined different outcome measures. Most notably, Fagan, Zimring, and Geller (2006) focused on all capital murders, and Frakes and Harding (2009) examined child murders which, depending on the state and year, may or may not be death penalty eligible. Otherwise, the key characteristics of these two studies are similar to the ones reviewed in this chapter. Interestingly, although both studies focused on the impact of the death penalty on capital eligible murders, Fagan, Zimring, and Geller found no evidence that the death penalty deters murder,

TABLE 4-1 Panel Studies Reviewed

Study	Legal Status	Intensity of Use	Use of an Instrument	Results: Sign[a] and Significance[b] of Point Estimates
Berk (2005)	N	Y	N	All possible results
Cohen-Cole et al. (2009)	Y	Y	Y	All possible results
Donohue and Wolfers (2005, 2009)	Y	Y	Y	All possible results
Dezhbakhsh and Shepherd (2006)	Y	Y	N	$-^{**}$
Dezhbakhsh, Rubin, and Shepherd (2003)[c]	Y	Y	Y	$-^{**}$; and $-^{NS}$
Katz, Levitt, and Shustorovich (2003)	N	Y	N	$-^{**}$; $-^{NS}$, and $+^{NS}$
Kovandzic, Vieraitis, and Boots (2009)	Y	Y	N	$-^{NS}$, $+^{NS}$
Mocan and Gittings (2003)	Y	Y	N	$-^{**}$; and $-^{NS}$
Mocan and Gittings (2010)	N	Y	N	$-^{**}$; and $-^{NS}$
Zimmerman (2004)	N	Y	Y	$-^{*}$; and $-^{NS}$

[a]Sign of the estimated coefficients: $-$, the estimated effect of capital sanctions on homicide is negative, indicating a deterrent effect; $+$, the estimated effect of capital sanctions on homicide is positive, indicating a brutalization effect.

[b]Statistical significance levels: NS, no statistical significance at $p = 0.05$; *, $p < 0.05$; **, $p < 0.01$.

[c]Dezhbakhsh, Rubin, and Shepherd (2003) estimate 55 different panel data regression models. In 49 of the models, the estimated effect of capital sanctions on homicide is negative and statistically significant; in 4, the estimates are negative and insignificant; and in 2, the estimates are positive and insignificant.

include every study of deterrence using panel data, but instead provides information on a set of influential studies that use the different approaches found in the research and that draw a wide range of different conclusions. Studies designed to illustrate the fragility of the results reports in the literature, namely, Donohue and Wolfers (2005, 2009) and Cohen-Cole et al. (2009), apply the same basic models and thus are included in our review.

The first study characteristic is how researchers specify the expected cost function of committing a capital homicide $f(Z_{it})$. At the most basic level, studies seek to determine the effect of changes in the legal status of the death penalty, changes in the intensity with which the death penalty is applied, or both. Most studies evaluated the intensity of use, but some also focused on the legal status of the death penalty. The specification of the death penalty variables in the panel models varies widely across the research and has been the focus of much debate. The different specifications assume that quite different aspects of the sanction regime are salient for would-be murderers. The research has demonstrated that different death penalty sanction variables, and different specifications of these variables, lead to very different deterrence estimates—negative and positive, large and small, both statistically significant and not statistically significant.

The second characteristic of interest is whether the death penalty measure is assumed to be randomly applied after controlling for the observed covariates and the fixed effects. The choice of whether or not to use instrumental variables, and the particular variables selected, has led to contentious differences in model assumptions invoked across the literature. In most of the studies, the researchers have assumed that the death penalty is unrelated to the unobserved factors associated with the homicide rate. That is, the unobserved factors, ε_{it}, are not associated with the death penalty sanctions. Studies using this independence assumption have drawn conflicting conclusions (see Table 4-1) with some reporting statistically significant evidence in favor of a deterrence effect, many others finding that capital punishment has a negative but statistically insignificant association with homicide, and a few others reporting evidence in favor of a brutalization effect, that capital punishment increases homicide.

Dezhbakhsh, Rubin, and Shepherd (2003) and Zimmerman (2004) argue that death penalty sanctions are likely to be correlated with unobserved determinants of homicide, and instead propose using instrumental variables to provide variation in the risk perceptions of potential murderers that is separable from the effects of all of the unobserved factors. The results of

---

and Frakes and Harding reported substantial deterrent effects. Our review does not consider the choice of the outcome variable: although this choice may have important implications for inference, these issues are secondary relative to the more fundamental issues covered in this chapter.

studies that do not use such instrumental variables vary from those that do, and the results of studies that use different instrumental variables vary from each other.

The fact that the estimated effects of the death penalty on homicide are sensitive to the different data and modeling assumptions used is not surprising. Deterrence estimates from the panel models depend on state changes over time in the legal status of the death penalty or the intensity with which the death penalty is applied. Since the moratorium was lifted, such changes have been few and far between (see Chapter 2). Because of the way in which the death penalty has been implemented in the United States in the last 30 years, no executions occur in most states in most years (86 percent of state-year observations), and when there are any, the number is almost always very low. In addition, the executions that do occur are concentrated in particular states, with Texas carrying out executions an order of magnitude more often than any other state. There also tends to be little variability for states over time in their numbers of or rates of executions and whether they legally allow executions. Only 11 states experienced one or more changes in legal status of the death penalty after the national moratorium was lifted. Overall, in recent decades in the United States the death penalty has been a rare practice that is concentrated in a few places.

Not only is there low variability in the application of the death penalty, there are only a small number of state-year observations that exhibit large variations in homicide rates over time. Figure 4-1 illustrates a partial regression plot with a death penalty sanction measure on the horizontal axis and the homicide rate on the vertical axis (adjusted for state and year fixed effects and typical covariates). This plot reflects the data, covariates, and specification used by Kovandzic, Vieraitis, and Boots (2009).[3] In displaying these regression results, the committee is not endorsing this or any other particular study.[4] Instead, our purpose is to illustrate how outlier or influential observations may affect regression results. Since the effect of the death penalty is estimated as the slope of the ordinary least squares regression line between the bulk of the data near zero and the location of the small set of influential values, the estimates in the research studies can vary widely (Berk, 2005). For example, if the particular state-year observations that are influential depend on the death penalty intensity measure used, then the slope of the regression line will vary with this measure. If one believes in the validity of the underlying model applied in Figure 4-1, then the outlier

---

[3]The execution measure is computed using the number of executions the year before the period year divided by the number of death sentences 7 years prior to the period year. For full model specification, see Figure 4-1 notes in the figure caption.

[4]In particular, we note that alternative but similar specifications result in a positive sloping, rather than a negative sloping line.

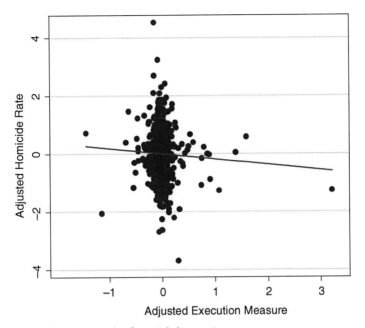

FIGURE 4-1 Illustration of influential data points.

NOTES: The plot reflects the data, covariates, and specification used by Kovandzic, Vieraitis, and Boots (2009), Table 3, Model 6 with the addition of two common sanction variables: death sentences divided by homicide arrests 2 years prior and homicide arrests divided by homicides. These additional variables required a measure of arrests for homicide, which was obtained from J. Wolfers' web page and was not available for years after 1998.

The horizontal axis represents the adjusted execution measure (residuals of execution measure regressed on all the rest of the regressors in the model). The execution measure is defined as the number of executions the prior year per number of death sentences 7 years prior, with missing values set to zero.

The vertical axis represents the adjusted homicide rate (residuals of the homicide rate regressed on all the regressors except the execution rate variable). The homicide rate is homicides per 100,000 residents. The regression was run on data for 1984-1998, weighted by state population share, and standard errors were clustered by state.

The coefficient of the ordinary least squares line between these two sets of adjusted variables—and hence the coefficient on the execution measure in the multiple linear regression of homicide rates on the execution measure and all covariates—is −0.183 (p = 0.173).

SOURCES: Data from T.V. Kovandzic (personal communication) and J. Wolfers. Wolfers' data are available at http://bpp.wharton.upenn.edu/jwolfers/DeathPenalty. shtml.

observations are informative. But if there is uncertainty about the validity of the model, the outliers can make the estimates highly sensitive to the underlying assumptions.

As noted in Chapter 2, the infrequency of executions does not mean that there is insufficient variation in the data to detect the effect of capital punishment. In fact, as shown in Table 4-1 (above), there is no shortage of statistically significant results reported in the literature. Rather, the problem is that inferences on the impact of the death penalty rest heavily on unsupported assumptions.

SPECIFYING THE EXPECTED COST OF COMMITTING A CAPITAL HOMICIDE: $f(Z_{it})$

In light of the variability in the estimated effects of the death penalty on homicide, a central question is whether the correct specification is being used and can be identified. We evaluate this question below by first focusing on measures of the perceived cost of murder and then taking up more generic issues associated with the panel data models in equation (4-1).

A vital component to evaluating the effect of the death penalty on homicide is to properly specify the expected cost function, $f(Z_{it})$, in Equation (4-1). Yet, researchers have failed to measure the relevant sanction regime and have relied on seemingly ad hoc measures of the relevant sanction probabilities.

What is the relevant treatment? Researchers have struggled to clearly specify and measure the incremental cost of a particular sanction policy. As noted in Chapter 3, there is little information on the sanction regime, and thus the counterfactual policy of interest. In particular, the research aims to determine the effect of an increase (or decrease) in the risk of receiving the death penalty or being executed relative not to *no* sanction, but rather relative to the other common sanctions for murder—lengthy prison sentences (with or without the possibility of parole). Moreover, these other aspects of the sanction regime may be changing over time, and any changes in the risks of the death penalty have to be evaluated relative to the varying but always higher risks associated with prison sentences. Two mechanisms that could plausibly create associations between changes in death penalty and prison sentence sanctions for homicide are the plea bargaining process, through which the threat of the death penalty may change the likelihood of sentences of different lengths, including life without parole, and the punitiveness of a state's culture, which influences the severity of the capital and noncapital aspects of the sanction regime.

None of the studies we reviewed made any use of information on other sanction risks for murder or the ways in which they may be changing over time. For this reason, it is not possible to tell if any "treatment" effects found in these models are due to death penalty sanction changes or to changes in other more frequently used sanctions that are part of a state's sanction regime for homicide. If changes in the death penalty are part of a larger "law and order" program, then concurrent changes in other much more heavily used sanctions could be at the root of any associated change in homicide rates.

A related problem in specifying a cost function is the ad hoc and inconsistent measures of subjective sanction probabilities. How do potential offenders measure the expected cost of committing a capital offense? The difficulty in answering this question stems from two interrelated problems: first, there is little information on how offenders perceive the relevant probabilities of arrest, conviction, and execution; and second, in practice, these probabilities may be difficult to measure.

In the studies we reviewed, one or both of just two features of the death penalty are assumed to be salient for deterring homicide: the legal status of the death penalty (in each state and year) and what are described as measures of the intensity with which the death penalty is applied (in each state and year). A variety of different and complex temporal structures are used to measure the probabilities of arrest, death sentence, and execution.

Consider, for example, the specifications used for variables described as the risk of execution given a death sentence:

- the number of executions in the prior year (prior to the current year's homicide rate);
- the number of executions in the prior year divided by the number of death sentences in the same prior year (or a variant, using a 12-month moving average of these counts for both the numerator and denominator);
- the number of executions in the current or prior year divided by the number of death sentences in an earlier prior year (3, 4, 5, 6, and 7 years prior have all been implemented and similar specifications using executions from the first three quarters of the current year and last quarter of prior year divided by death sentences 6 years prior);
- the number of executions in the prior year divided by the number of death row inmates in the prior year;
- the number of executions in the current year divided by the number of homicides in the prior year;
- the number of executions in the prior year divided by the number of prisoners in the prior year (or 2 or 3 years prior); and
- the number of executions in the prior year divided by the population of the state in the prior year.

There is no empirical basis for choosing among these specifications, and there has been heated debate among researchers about them, particularly on the number of years that should be lagged for the numerator and, even more so, for the denominator in order to best correspond to the relevant risk of execution given a death sentence in each state and year.

This debate, however, is not based on clear and principled arguments as to why the probability timing that is used corresponds to the objective probability of execution, or, even more importantly, to criminal perceptions of that probability. Instead, researchers have constructed ad hoc measures of criminal perceptions. Consequently, the results have proven to be highly sensitive to the specific measures used. Donohue and Wolfers (2005) find, for example, that when reanalyzing the results in Mocan and Gittings (2003), using a 7-year lag implies that the death penalty deters homicide (4.4 lives saved per execution) but using a 1-year lag implies that the death penalty increases the number of homicides (1.2 lives lost per execution). Donohue and Wolfers (2005) question whether would-be murderers are aware of the number of death sentences handed down 7 years prior. Responding to these concerns, Mocan and Gittings (2010) argue that because executions do not take place the same year as a sentence is imposed, models with a 1-year lag are meaningless.

Whether any of these measures accurately reflect the relevant risk probabilities is uncertain. The basic problem is that little is known about how those who may commit murder perceive the sanctions for this crime. If the death penalty is going to have an effect on the behavior of this group, it is their perceptions of the sanction regime for murder that matter. It is not known whether the current legal status of the death penalty is salient to potential murderers; other relevant factors could include how often the legal status of the death penalty has changed in recent years and the presence of high-profile cases, which create greater awareness of the legality of the death penalty in a state. Similarly, it is not known whether specific state and year information is salient to potential murderers; no evidence or theory is presented in the studies we reviewed to argue that the particular measures are valid or that alternative measures—such as executions in surrounding states or in one's own county or executions in the last 5 years or the last 3 months—are not equally valid. As potential murderers may be attempting to predict the effective sanction regime several or many years into the future, when they might be sentenced or executed, it is particularly unclear what the relevant geographic or time horizon is for obtaining a salient measure.

Suppose that when deciding whether to commit a crime, potential murderers weigh the benefits and risks that committing murder may bring them along with the likelihood of those benefits or risks occurring. In this setting, the probability of being sentenced to death and henceforth being executed are theorized to be among these perceived risks. The sanction risks are necessarily based on the individual's perceptions. Either implicitly or explicitly, researchers in this field typically make an additional assumption that the risk perceptions of potential murderers are accurate and thus the *perceived risks* of receiving a death sentence, being executed, or being executed within a particular time period, are equivalent to the *objective measures* of these risks. The accuracy of this assertion that the risk perceptions of potential murderers are correct is questionable. There is no clear enforcement mechanism or learning process that would create such accuracy over time in potential murderers' perceptions of the risk of incurring the death penalty.

Even if potential murderers' risk perceptions are accurate, researchers must carefully specify the probabilities that might affect behavior and must confront the practical difficulties involved in measuring the relevant probabilities. The studies to date, however, have failed to address either of these issues. Because the post-*Gregg* panel research has not developed models based on the potential offender's decision problem, the studies may mis-specify the relevant risk probabilities.

Much of this research considers how different conditional probabilities—say, the probability of execution given capital sanctions—each *separately* affects behavior (see, e.g., Dezhbakhsh, Rubin, and Shepherd, 2003). Yet, in standard decision models in which potential offenders weigh the uncertain benefits and costs of committing a crime, the joint probability of execution, capital sanctions, and arrests are germane. In this expected utility framework, Durlauf, Navarro, and Rivers (2010) show that the effect of the conditional probability of execution given a death sentence cannot be understood separately from the effects of the conditional probability of being caught and being sentenced to death if caught. Moreover, under a rational choice assumption, what will matter is the expected execution rate at time t + 6, which is not necessarily equal to the t − 6 years used in the literature.

Aside from this important issue of modeling and functional form, researchers also encounter practical obstacles in measuring the objective risks. Consider the risk of being executed given a death sentence, the risk that has been most focused on in the research, and consider how this risk could be objectively measured and updated each year for those in each state, as is assumed relevant in these models. In 1977, the first full year after the *Gregg* decision, 31 states provided the legal authority to impose the death penalty. In 1977, there were no data on the actual use of the death penalty in any state to create an estimate of the risk of execution. Some people might have predicted that Texas would be more vigorous in its actual use of the death penalty than California or Pennsylvania, but there were as yet no data to confirm such a prediction. Thus, it is unclear what the objective risk of receiving a death sentence or consequently being executed was in any state for which the death penalty was legal in 1977. Only over time could an objective risk be based on data. Thus, over time one would expect divergent risks to develop in different states as data on the actual use of the death penalty in each state accumulated.

The process of forming and revising objective measures of the risks associated with the death penalty, however, would then be complicated by additional factors. One is that the volume of data on death sentences and executions available for calculating estimates of risk depends on the size of the state. By various measures of execution risk reported in Chapter 2, Delaware was at least as aggressive in its use of the death penalty as Texas. However, over the period from 1976 to 2000, Delaware sentenced 28 people to death and carried out 11 executions, while Texas sentenced 753 people to death and carried out 231 executions. Thus, potential murderers have far more data on the actual practice of capital punishment each year in Texas than in Delaware. As a consequence, even for well-informed potential murderers living in states with similar sanction regimes, one would expect sanction risk perceptions to evolve along different paths that would depend, among other things, on the size of the state.

Perhaps in an environment in which sanction regimes were plausibly stable, the objective risk of execution could be precisely estimated even in small states with low murder rates. However, sanction regimes do not appear to be uniformly stable in large states for which it is feasible to obtain precise measures of year-to-year variation. Indeed, it is changes in the sanction regime for murder that the panel models use to inform their estimates of deterrence. Moratoriums and commutations may signal changes in regimes, particularly when accompanied by high-visibility announcements such as that by former Illinois Governor George Ryan in 2000. As noted in Chapter 2, Texas appears to have shifted to a higher intensity execution sanction regime during the 1990s. Thus, in an environment in which sanction regimes are changing, the value of older data in forming a correct estimate of the prevailing sanction regime deteriorates. Moreover, the value of current data in forming a correct estimate of the future sanction regime also deteriorates. This forecast is particularly relevant as those considering murder now would face the sanction regime of the state in which the homicide is prosecuted some significant time in the future. These factors raise the question of whether year-to-year variation in a measure, such as the number of people executed in a state, has any bearing on the risk of execution for someone committing a murder today. Overall, the degree to which this, or other proposed measures of execution risk, predicts later executions has not been established.

To illustrate the problems associated with these different measures, consider using the number of executions in a state 1 year prior to the year in which the homicide rate is measured divided by the number of death sentences in that state 7 years earlier. Those at risk for execution in any particular year are all those on death row at some point in that year. Those who were sentenced to death 7 years earlier could be executed at any time after their sentence, with different probabilities of being executed in each year based on the particulars of their crime, the appeals process, their health, the current governor, etc. In the early years after the national death penalty moratorium ended, on a national level, those who were executed had spent an average of 6-7 years on death row (Snell, 2010). There are several problems with using this information to justify lagging the denominator of a risk of execution measure by 7 years. First, only 15 percent of those sentenced to death in the United States since 1977 have been executed, with close to 40 percent leaving death row for other reasons (vacated sentences or convictions, commutations, a successful appeal, or death by other causes), and 45 percent are still on death row (Snell, 2010). Moreover, these figures vary substantially across states and over time.

Table 4-2 displays the number of inmates removed from death row in each state by the reasons for removal. First, there is substantial variation in the execution rates across states. For example, of the 150 people in Virginia sentenced to death from 1973 to 2009, 105—70 percent—have been executed. In contrast, in North Carolina, only 8 percent of the 528 people sentenced to death have been executed. Not only do these rates vary across states, but they also vary over time (see, e.g., Cook, 2009). Clearly, the number of years those executed have spent on death row is not an accurate measure of the number of years those on death row will spend there before they are executed, if they are ever executed. Second, the time spent on death row by those executed has varied over time at the national level, and it varies considerably by state (Snell, 2010). Third, no evidence has been given or arguments made to suggest that death sentences that come to some resolution earlier than others are indicative of the resolution for death sentences that have not yet come to resolution. Thus, using a fixed number of years of lag between those sentenced and those executed means that for many states and years this lag will have an uncertain relationship to the objective risk of execution given a death sentence.

The fact that there is a mismatch between the numerator and denominator in the models used is perhaps best illustrated by the many state-year cases in which there are one or more executions the prior year but there were no death sentences imposed 7 years earlier. Researchers have made a variety of ad hoc removals or substitutions for these undefined cases including: replace with zero or treat as missing (Kovandzic, Vieraitis, and Boots, 2009); numerator set to zero regardless of denominator and non-zero numerator and zero denominator considered missing at random (Donohue and Wolfers, 2005; Mocan and Gittings, 2003, 2010); replace with most

TABLE 4-2 Death Sentences and Removals, by Jurisdiction and Reason for Removal, 1973-2009

Jurisdiction	Total Sentenced to Death, 1973-2009	Removals Executed	Removals Died	Sentence or Conviction Overturned	Sentence Commuted	Other Removals	Under Sentence of Death, December 31, 2009
U.S. Total	8,115	1,188	416	2,939	365	34	3,173
Federal	65	3	0	6	1	0	55
Alabama	412	44	31	135	2	0	200
Arizona	286	23	14	110	7	1	131
Arkansas	110	27	3	38	2	0	40
California	927	13	73	142	15	0	684
Colorado	21	1	2	15	1	0	2
Connecticut	13	1	0	2	0	0	10
Delaware	56	14	0	25	0	0	17
Florida	977	68	53	447	18	2	389
Georgia	320	46	16	147	9	1	101
Idaho	42	1	3	21	3	0	14
Illinois	307	12	15	96	156	12	16
Indiana	100	20	4	54	6	2	14
Kansas	12	0	0	3	0	0	9
Kentucky	81	3	6	35	2	0	35
Louisiana	238	27	6	114	7	1	83
Maryland	53	5	3	36	4	0	5
Massachusetts	4	0	0	2	2	0	0

Mississippi	190	10	5	112	0	3	60
Missouri	182	67	10	52	2	0	51
Montana	15	3	2	6	2	0	2
Nebraska	32	3	4	12	2	0	11
Nevada	147	12	15	36	4	0	80
New Hampshire	1	0	0	0	0	0	1
New Jersey	52	0	3	33	8	8	0
New Mexico	28	1	1	19	5	0	2
New York	10	0	0	10	0	0	0
North Carolina	528	43	21	297	8	0	159
Ohio	401	33	20	168	15	0	165
Oklahoma	350	91	12	165	3	0	79
Oregon	58	2	2	23	0	0	31
Pennsylvania	399	3	24	148	6	0	218
Rhode Island	2	0	0	2	0	0	0
South Carolina	203	42	5	98	3	0	55
South Dakota	5	1	1	1	0	0	2
Tennessee	221	6	15	105	4	2	89
Texas	1,040	447	38	167	56	1	331

continued

TABLE 4-2 Continued

Jurisdiction	Total Sentenced to Death, 1973-2009	Removals		Sentence or Conviction Overturned	Sentence Commuted	Other Removals	Under Sentence of Death, December 31, 2009
		Executed	Died				
Utah	27	6	1	9	1	0	10
Virginia	150	105	6	14	11	1	13
Washington	38	4	1	25	0	0	8
Wyoming	12	1	1	9	0	0	1
Percentage	100	14.6	5.1	36.2	4.5	0.4	39.1

NOTE: Some inmates executed since 1977 or currently under sentences of death were sentenced prior to 1977. For those inmates sentenced to death more than once, the numbers are based on the most recent death sentence.
SOURCE: Snell (2010), Table 20.

recent defined ratio (Zimmerman, 2004). These (and other) ad hoc adjustments highlight the general problem that the people who were sentenced to death 7 years earlier may be executed before or after the year in which executions are counted, and they are not the only people at risk for being executed in the current or prior year. Overall, the interpretation of this ratio is not clear at all, whether the denominator is lagged any particular number of years, and its relevance to the objective risk of execution for each state and year, let alone to the risk perceptions of potential murderers, is highly questionable.

Basing execution risk measures only on data on executions that have actually been carried out, as has been done in the research being discussed, could result in a serious underestimate of the eventual probability of execution for those given a death sentence. In addition, this fact raises serious questions about whether the risk of *ever* being executed after a death sentence is the most salient measure or whether additional information is salient, such as measures that consider expected time to death, expected living conditions while on death row, and in comparison, expected time to death during a long prison sentence and conditions while in prison in that state. (Of course, one can only speculate about which, if any, of these variables is salient for potential murderers.)

These many complications make clear that even with a concerted effort by dedicated researchers to assemble and analyze relevant data on death sentences and executions, assessment of the actual and changing objective risk of execution that faces a potential murderer is a daunting challenge. Given the obstacles to obtaining an objective measure of this risk, the committee does not find any of the measures used in the studies to be credible measures of the objective risk of execution given a death sentence. We also reiterate that it is not known whether there is a relationship between any of these measures or any more credible objective measure of execution risk, and the execution risk as perceived by potential murderers.

MODEL ASSUMPTIONS

The conceptual and measurement concerns raised thus far, which are somewhat unique to studies on the effects of the death penalty on homicides, make it difficult to even to envision how one could draw valid inferences on the deterrent effect using the existing data. There is a complete lack of basic information on the noncapital component of the sanction regime, on how offenders perceive sanction risks, and on how to accurately measure those risks.

Even if these measurement problems are some day fully addressed, all studies using observational data must also address the counterfactual outcomes problem that arises because the data cannot reveal the outcome that would occur if the death penalty had not been applied in treatment states and had been applied in control states. The data alone cannot reveal the effect of the death penalty. Rather, researchers must combine data with assumptions.

In the studies we reviewed, variations of the model in Equation 1 have been used to identify the impact of the death penalty on homicide. In this section, we consider the credibility of the four assumptions that have been applied in this literature: (1) that the death penalty measures are independent of the unobserved factors influencing homicide; (2) that certain observed covariates, called instrumental variables, are correlated with the death penalty but not with the unobserved factors that influence homicide; (3) that the effect of the death penalty is the same for all states and years; and (4) that the sanction regimes of adjacent states do not have any bearing on the effect of the death penalty in a particular state. We begin with a brief discussion of the benefits of random assignment.

Benefits of Random Assignment

As discussed in Chapter 3, random assignment of treatment to large samples of subjects leads the distributions of all other characteristics of treatment and control subjects, whether observed or unobserved, to be approximately the same across the two groups. With small samples of subjects, this feature will hold on average, meaning that if a given set of subjects is repeatedly randomly assigned to treatment or control conditions, then the features of the subjects over all possible treatment groups and all possible controls groups would be exactly equal. In any particular randomization, however, there may be some features that differ by chance for the subjects in the treatment condition and those in the control condition.

This "balancing" of the characteristics of treatment and control subjects justifies the attribution of any difference in outcomes between the treatment and control groups to the treatment and not to other factors that may differ between the treatment and control subjects. Without randomization, the threat of misattributing the cause of any observed differences in outcomes to the treatment when it is actually due to other factors that differ between the groups is always present. In the remainder of this section we focus on the specific challenges this concern raises with regard to the death penalty and deterrence research, discuss the methodological strategies proposed to overcome these challenges, and assess whether these strategies have been successful.

In research on the death penalty and deterrence, the sanction regime for murder (including the legal status of the death penalty and the intensity with which the death penalty is applied) is, for obvious reason, not randomly assigned to state-by-year units. Hence, the possibility is present that other factors may be the actual causes of any changes seen in homicide rates. Mechanically, what is required for this misattribution to occur is for death penalty changes to occur at similar times and places as changes in the true underlying causal factors. An example is a shift to a political leader with a "law and order" approach, which could both increase death-penalty-related risks and increase the perceived or actual arrest rates, either or both of which could bring down the homicide rate.

Fixed Effect Regression Model

Two methodological strategies are used to try to identify changes in the homicide rate that are caused by changes in the sanction regime for murder and not by other factors. The first methodological strategy is a fixed effect multiple regression (described above), in which fixed state and year effects are used to account for unobserved determinants of homicide. Given these fixed effects, researchers assume that the death penalty measures are statistically independent of the unobserved determinants of homicide, as would be the case in a randomized experiment. The second methodological strategy is to add an instrumental variables analysis to the fixed effect multiple regression models.

The fixed effects multiple regression models rely on state level variation in death penalty measures over time to attempt to identify a causal effect of death-penalty-related changes on homicide after controlling for the effects of the other variables in the models. But even if one provisionally assumes that the death penalty measures used in these models are correctly specified (i.e., are the salient factors for potential murderers), that the state-year unit is the unit at which potential murderers are assessing death-penalty-associated risks, and that the specification of all other variables and of the functional form of the model are correct, additional strong assumptions are still required for panel models to deliver estimates of a deterrent effect of the death penalty.

In the fixed effect models, states that do not apply the death penalty sanction are used to estimate the missing counterfactual for states that do experience different death penalty sanction levels. This approach identifies a causal effect only if there are no other factors besides the death penalty causing homicide rates to change differently in states that do and do not experience changes in death penalty sanctions. Many such factors may well exist—such as changes in economic conditions, crime rates, public perceptions or political regimes—and there is no reason to believe that these variables are fixed over time or across states. Moreover, the committee considers the omission from these models of other changes in the sanction regime for murder especially problematic. As discussed above, other changes in the sanction regime for murder, such as the likelihood of life without parole or the average sentence length, may well change concurrently with death-penalty-related changes and so affect homicide rates. If states that do not experience changes in the death penalty also did not experience comparable changes (on average) in other aspects of the sanction regime for murder, then the required assumption is violated, and those states cannot provide the missing counterfactual information for states that do experience changes in the death penalty.

A related concern is that while death penalty sanctions may be affecting the homicide rate, the homicide rate may also be affecting death penalty sanctions and statutes. Since factors causing changes in observed in death penalty sanctions are unknown, one cannot rule out that changes in the homicide rate are among such factors. One way this could occur is that an increase in homicides may influence policy makers to increase the seriousness of sanctions or the likelihood of more serious sanctions for murder. Given this possibility, it is interesting to note that states in an available sanction have higher homicide rates on average than states that do not have the death penalty. Alternatively, an increase in the homicide rate may decrease the intensity with which the death penalty is applied as death penalty proceedings require more resources than non-death-penalty proceedings (Alarcón and Mitchell, 2011; California Commission on the Fair Administration of Justice, 2008; Cook, 2009; Roman, Chalfin, and Knight, 2009). This potential reverse causality problem—termed simultaneity in econometrics and feedback from output to input in the literature on causality—is particularly thorny to overcome. It was a major concern of the earlier National Research Council (1978) report on deterrence.

Instrumental Variables

In light of these concerns, Dezhbakhsh, Rubin, and Shepherd (2003) and Zimmerman (2004) have added an additional identification strategy, the use of instrumental variables. The idea behind an instrument is to separate out the part of any observed relationship between the death penalty and homicide that is spurious (i.e., resulting from the relationship of both to other factors) from the part of the relationship between the death penalty and homicide that is causal. The success of an instrument and the consequent instrumental variables analysis depends on the ability of the instrument to identify the portion of the variation in the treatment that is not contaminated by other causal factors that covary with the treatment and affect the outcome.

The success of an instrument depends on the degree to which it meets two requirements: (1) the death penalty sanction must vary with the value of the instrument, and (2) the average outcome must *not* vary as a function of the value of the instrument conditional on the treatment and levels of other covariates. A sufficient condition for this to hold is that the instrument affects the homicide rate only through its effect on the death penalty sanctions, that is, that the instrument has no direct effect of its own on homicide rates. The first of these requirements can be checked empirically. The second requirement typically cannot be established using data and empirical analysis; it requires, instead, logic or theory to establish its credibility.

In the studies of death penalty and deterrence, the challenge is to find a variable that predicts death penalty sanctions but does not have a direct effect on the homicide rate. Although successful instrumental variables are notoriously difficult to come up with, making an argument for a particular instrument in this setting is complicated by the same fact that makes a spurious correlation very difficult to rule out. Little is known about the factors that actually affect homicide rates and, thus, the relevant factors may not be observed, measured, and controlled for. Compounding the problem, even less is known about factors that are associated with death-penalty-related-changes in the sanction regime for murder, or more relevantly, changes in perceptions of sanction risks. As noted above, factors contributing to changes in the legal status of the death penalty or the intensity with which the death penalty is applied could include economic, crime, or political changes that may also have direct consequences for the homicide rate.

These two gaps in knowledge—of factors that contribute to the homicide rate and factors that contribute to changes in the legality or practice of the death penalty and of risk perceptions—combine to heighten the concern that any association observed between death penalty changes and homicide rate changes may well be due to other factors. Thus, it is particularly difficult to convincingly establish that a proposed instrument does not directly affect the homicide rate, as is required.

A couple of examples of credible instruments in other settings may be useful to compare with those proposed in the studies of the death penalty and deterrence. In studies of crime and justice, Lee and McCrary (2009) use the age at which an offender can be tried as an adult as an instrument to identify the deterrent effect of incarceration; and Klick and Tabarrok (2005) use terror alerts in Washington, DC, as an instrument to identify the deterrent effect of police on crime on the Washington Mall. In the field of labor economics, a person's Vietnam draft number has been used as an instrument to identify the effect of military service on future earnings because one's draft number affects military service but does not have any direct effect on future earnings (Angrist, 1990). Month of birth has been used as an instrument to identify the effect of number of years of schooling on earnings because month of birth affects the academic year in which high school students of similar ages may legally leave school, but it is unlikely to have any direct effect on earnings (Angrist and Kreuger, 1991).

In contrast, the instruments proposed in the panel studies of the death penalty often appear to clearly violate the second requirement and sometimes violate the first. The instruments that have been used include police payroll, judicial expenditures, Republican vote share in each separate presidential election, prison admissions, the proportion of a state's murders in which the assailant and victim are strangers, the proportion of a state's murders that are nonfelony, the proportion of murders by nonwhite offenders, an indicator (yes/no) for whether there were any releases from death row due to a vacated sentence, and an indicator (yes/no) for whether there was a botched execution. The specific death penalty variables for which these instruments are proposed are measures of the risk for murderers of being arrested, the risk for those arrested for murder of receiving a death sentence, and the risk for those receiving a death sentence of being executed.

The studies offer very little justification for why these instruments are believed to be unrelated to the unobserved determinants of homicide, and in many cases the committee does not find the assumptions to be credible. To take two examples, it seems highly unlikely that police expenditures or the Republican vote share in a particular presidential election affect homicide rates only through the intensity with which the death penalty is exercised. To the contrary, police expenditures are likely to have a direct effect on homicide rates, and Republican vote shares may be related to a host of factors that are thought to influence crime (e.g., "get tough on crime" policies and a state's demographic composition).

The idea of using instrumental variables to help identify the effect of the death penalty on homicides is sensible. The problem, however, is finding variables that are related to the sanction regime but not directly related to homicide rates. In general, the committee finds that the instruments proposed in the research are not credible and, as a result, this identification strategy has thus far failed to overcome the challenges to identifying a causal effect of the death penalty on homicide rates.[5]

Homogeneity

Still another assumption of the panel regression model in Equation (4-1) is that any effect that the death penalty has on homicide rates is the same

---

[5]In addition to these fundamental problems with the instruments, Donohue and Wolfers (2005) document that the results are highly sensitive to the specification of the instruments. For example, the results of Dezhbakhsh, Rubin, and Shepherd (2003) notably vary depending on whether and how one specifies the Republican vote share instrument: when using vote shares from six different elections, Dezhbakhsh, Rubin, and Shepherd (2003) report that each additional execution saves an average of 18 lives; when using a single vote share measure from the most recent election, Donohue and Wolfers (2005, p. 826) find that "instead of saving eighteen lives, each execution leads to eighteen lives *lost*." Moreover, Donohue and Wolfers find that when the partisanship variables are not included among the instruments, more executions lead to substantially *more* homicides.

in every state and every year. This assumption of a *homogeneous treatment effect* is unlikely to hold in practice. This assumption relies on "unit exchangeability," which requires that if the change in the death penalty measure observed in a particular state and year were instead to be observed in a different state and year, then the effect seen on homicide would be the same. For the legal status of the death penalty, this assumption would mean that the death penalty would have the same effect on homicides in the first year a low-crime state instituted the death penalty by legislative action as it would in the 15th year in Texas, a state in which it is widely used. The assumption would also mean that the effect would be the same in the year before the death penalty was removed as a possible sanction due to the courts' determining the state's death penalty law was unconstitutional in a state that had the death penalty but did not implement it. The death-penalty-intensity models also invoke this assumption. These models assume that every possible death-penalty-intensity level would have the same effect on homicide rates in every state and year if it was present in that state and year, regardless of the prior sanction regime, a state's history with the death penalty, or any other factor.

Although this homogeneity assumption is commonly invoked in regression models, no support is offered for it in studies of the death penalty, and on its face it appears unlikely to hold. In fact, there is some evidence to the contrary. Figure 4-2 displays the distribution of estimates found by Donohue and Wolfers (2005, p. 810, Figure 4) when they estimate state-specific parameters using the same basic specification as in Dezhbakhsh and Shepherd (2006). They find that reinstatement of the death penalty in 1976 is associated with an increased homicide rate in 17 states and a lower rate in 24 states. Similarly, when Shepherd (2005) estimated state-specific deterrence parameters using the same basic specifications as in Dezhbakhsh, Rubin, and Shepherd (2003), she finds that executions deterred murder in 8 states, and increased murders in 13 states. The committee does not endorse these state-specific models and estimates, but the findings do suggest the potential for substantial heterogeneity in the effect of the death penalty across states, which violates a basic assumption of the panel data model in Equation (4-1). Moreover, relaxing this homogeneity assumption can lead to very different inferences on the effect of the death penalty (see Chapter 6).

Finally, we note that the panel regression models also rely on the assumption that the sanction regimes of adjacent states do not have any bearing on the effect the death penalty in a particular state. In other words, the assumption asserts that the effect of the legalization of death penalty (or an increase to a higher death-penalty-intensity level) is the same for a state regardless of whether it is surrounded by states with a death penalty that is rarely implemented or is adjacent to, say, Texas. Although it is possible that the legal status of the death penalty (or an increase to a higher death-

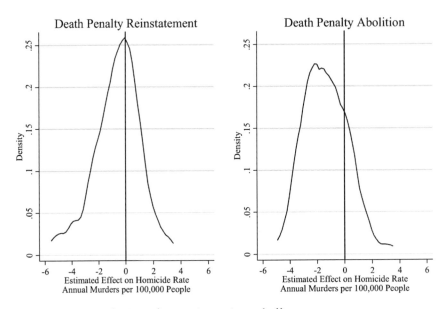

FIGURE 4-2 Distribution of regression-estimated effects across states.
SOURCE: Donohue and Wolfers (2005, p. 810, Figure 4). Used by permission.

penalty-intensity level) may have the same effect in each of these scenarios, it is also plausible that in the first setting the change in the sanction regime for murder would be perceived as small to potential murderers and in the second it would seem large. No research to date has explored whether the assumption that the treatment effect is insensitive to context created by other states is likely to hold, but violations of this assumption are known to lead to biased inferences (see, e.g., Rubin, 1986, p. 961). While accounting for social interactions is known to be difficult, Manski (in press) points to constructive ways of further addressing some of the problems that have been identified in the research to date.

CONCLUSION

The committee finds the failure of the panel studies we reviewed to address or overcome the primary challenges discussed above sufficient reason to view this research as noninformative with regard to the effect of the death penalty on homicides. The sanction regime is insufficiently specified and the measures of the intensity with which the death penalty is applied are flawed. No connection has been established between these measures and the perceived sanction risks of potential murderers. Neither the fixed effects multiple regression models nor the proposed instruments are credible in overcoming challenges to identifying a causal link between the death penalty and homicide rates. The homogeneous response restriction that the effects are the same for all states and all time periods seems patently not credible.

Some researchers have argued that fixed effect models without instruments may provide valuable information, although not perfect information about the impact of death penalty on crime. One reason given is that they do not suffer from the defects that attend the use of manifestly invalid instrumental variables (see, for example, Donohue and Wolfers, 2009, and Kovandzic, Vieraitis, and Boots, 2009). This assessment of the informative value of the fixed effects models is dubious for several reasons. Most notably, these models do not address the data and modeling issues discussed throughout this chapter. The fixed effects models estimated in the literature do not specify the noncapital component of the sanction regime and setting aside the issue of how sanction risks are actually perceived, the measures of execution risk that are used do not appear to bear any resemblance to the true risk of execution. In addition, the key assumption that the death penalty sanction is independent of other unobserved factors that might influence homicide rates seems untenable. For these reasons, the fixed effects models are no more informative about the effect of the death penalty on homicide rates than other types of model.

Some studies play the useful role, either intentionally or not, of demonstrating the fragility of claims to have or not to have found deterrent effects (e.g., see Cohen-Cole et al., 2009; Donohue and Wolfers, 2005, 2009). However, even these studies suffer from the intrinsic shortcomings that severely limit what can be learned about the effect of the death penalty on homicide rates by using data on the death penalty as it has actually been administered in the United States in the past 35 years.

The challenges discussed here are formidable, and breakthroughs on several fronts would be necessary to overcome them. Only then might panel models, with or without instruments, be a fruitful methodology for studying the deterrent effects associated with the death penalty.

REFERENCES

Alarcón, A.L., and Mitchell, P.M. (2011). Executing the will of the voters?: A roadmap to mend or end the California legislature's multibillion-dollar death penalty debacle. *Loyola of Los Angeles Law Review, 44*(Special), S41-S224.

Angrist, J.D. (1990). Lifetime earnings and the Vietnam era draft lottery: Evidence from Social Security administrative records. *American Economic Review, 80*(3), 313-336.

Angrist, J.D., and Krueger, A.B. (1991). Does compulsory school attendance affect schooling and earnings? *The Quarterly Journal of Economics, 106*(4), 979-1,014.

Berk, R. (2005). New claims about executions and general deterrence: Déjà vu all over again? *Journal of Empirical Legal Studies, 2*(2), 303-330.

California Commission on the Fair Administration of Justice. (2008). *Report and Recommendations on the Administration of the Death Penalty in California.* Sacramento: Author.

Cohen-Cole, E., Durlauf, S., Fagan, J., and Nagin, D. (2009). Model uncertainty and the deterrent effect of capital punishment. *American Law and Economics Review, 11*(2), 335-369.

Cook, P.J. (2009). Potential savings from abolition of the death penalty in North Carolina. *American Law and Economics Review, 11*(2), 498-529.

Dezhbakhsh, H., and Shepherd, J.M. (2006). The deterrent effect of capital punishment: Evidence from a "judicial experiment." *Economic Inquiry, 44*(3), 512-535.

Dezhbakhsh, H., Rubin, P.H., and Shepherd, J.M. (2003). Does capital punishment have a deterrent effect? New evidence from postmoratorium panel data. *American Law and Economics Review, 5*(2), 344-376.

Donohue, J.J., and Wolfers, J. (2005). Uses and abuses of empirical evidence in the death penalty debate. *Stanford Law Review, 58*(3), 791-845.

Donohue, J.J., and Wolfers, J. (2009). Estimating the impact of the death penalty on murder. *American Law and Economics Review, 11*(2), 249-309.

Durlauf, S., Navarro, S., and Rivers, D.A. (2010). Understanding aggregate crime regressions. *Journal of Econometrics, 158*(2), 306-317.

Fagan, J., Zimring, F.E., and Geller, A. (2006). Capital punishment and capital murder: Market share and the deterrent effects of the death penalty. *Texas Law Review, 84*(7), 1,803-1,867.

Frakes, M., and Harding, M.C. (2009). The deterrent effect of death penalty eligibility: Evidence from the adoption of child murder eligibility factors. *American Law and Economics Review, 11*(2), 451-497.

Katz, L., Levitt, S.D., and Shustorovich, E. (2003). Prison conditions, capital punishment, and deterrence. *American Law and Economics Review, 5*(2), 318-343.

Klick, J., and Tabarrok, A. (2005). Using terror alert levels to estimate the effect of police on crime. *Journal of Law & Economics, 48*(1), 267-279.

Kovandzic, T.V., Vieraitis, L.M., and Boots, D.P. (2009). Does the death penalty save lives? *Criminology & Public Policy, 8*(4), 803-843.

Lee, D., and McCrary, J. (2009). *The Deterrent Effect of Prison: Dynamic Theory and Evidence.* Unpublished paper. Industrial Relations Section, Department of Economics, Princeton University. Available: http://emlab.berkeley.edu/~jmccrary/lee_and_mccrary2009.pdf [December 2010].

Manski, C.F. (in press). Identification of treatment response with social interactions. Submitted to *The Econometrics Journal.* Available: http://onlinelibrary.wiley.com/doi/10.1111/j.1368-423X.2011.00368.x/abstract [December 2010].

Mocan, H.N., and Gittings, R.K. (2003). Getting off death row: Commuted sentences and the deterrent effect of capital punishment. *Journal of Law & Economics, 46*(2), 453-478.

Mocan, H.N., and Gittings, R.K. (2010). The impact of incentives on human behavior: Can we make it disappear? The case of the death penalty. In R.E.S. Di Tella and E. Schargrodsky (Eds.), *The Economics of Crime: Lessons for and from Latin America* (pp. 379-420). National Bureau of Economic Research conference report. Chicago: University of Chicago Press.

National Research Council. (1978). *Deterrence and Incapacitation: Estimating the Effects of Criminal Sanctions on Crime Rates.* Panel on Research on Deterrent and Incapacitative Effects. A. Blumstein, J. Cohen, and D. Nagin (Eds.), Committee on Research on Law Enforcement and Criminal Justice. Assembly of Behavioral and Social Sciences. Washington, DC: National Academy Press.

Roman, J.K., Chalfin, A.J., and Knight, C.R. (2009). Reassessing the cost of the death penalty using quasi-experimental methods: Evidence from Maryland. *American Law and Economics Review, 11*(2), 530-574.

Rubin, D.B. (1986). Statistics and causal inference: Comment: Which ifs have causal answers. *Journal of the American Statistical Association, 81*(396), 961-962.

Shepherd, J.M. (2005). Deterrence versus brutalization: Capital punishment's differing impacts among states. *Michigan Law Review, 104*(2), 203-255.

Snell, T.L. (2010). *Capital Punishment, 2009—Statistical Tables.* Report, U.S. Department of Justice (NCJ 231676). Available: http://www.ojp.usdoj.gov/index.cfm?ty=pbdetail& iid=2215. [December 2010].

Zimmerman, P.R. (2004). State executions, deterrence, and the incidence of murder. *Journal of Applied Economics, 7*(1), 163-193.

5

Time-Series Studies

Time-series studies of the effect of capital punishment on homicides study the statistical association of executions and homicides over time. As noted in the preceding chapter, panel studies also contain a time dimension, so the division between the two approaches is not perfect. Indeed, time-series studies can be thought of as a particular type of panel study, characterized by a small number of cross-sectional units, often only one or two. Some time-series studies analyze executions and homicides over a large number of periods; others examine the aftermath of single execution events. Whatever the length of the series, the intuition undergirding the analysis is that the presence of an effect of executions on homicide rates can be seen from the association of fluctuations of executions over time with fluctuations of homicides over time.

The time-series and panel studies we reviewed differ in several other important respects.

- First, the unit of time in time-series studies is usually months, weeks, or even days; in contrast, the unit of time in panel studies is usually a year. Thus, results from time-series studies are generally interpreted as measuring short-term effects of capital punishment.
- Second, time-series studies generally examine the association between execution events and homicides; panel studies generally measure the association of homicide rates with ratios that are intended to measure the probability of execution.

- Third, while most panel studies use very similar regression methods, time-series studies use a wide assortment of specialized time series methods.
- Fourth, the designs of time-series studies are more varied than are those of panel studies. Perhaps the most important difference among time-series studies is the number of execution events examined. Some time-series research focuses on the effect of a single execution event, and other studies combine data on many execution events and analyze their temporal association with homicide rates in a single statistical model.

The variation of research methods in the time-series studies makes it challenging to organize a cohesive discussion of the subject. It also is challenging to describe and critique the studies in a way that is understandable to audiences who do not have expertise in time-series methods. Methods for analysis of time-series data are specialized and often very technical. We address the second challenge by beginning this chapter with a nontechnical discussion of some relatively transparent problems of the studies. We then continue with further criticisms that of necessity are more technical.

BASIC CONCEPTUAL ISSUES

Execution Event Studies

Studies of single execution events attempt to identify whether a change in the homicide rate occurs in the immediate aftermath of a single execution. A decline is interpreted as evidence of deterrence; an increase is interpreted as evidence of a brutalization effect, whereby state-sanctioned executions "legitimate" homicide to some in the citizenry. If either such effect could be convincingly demonstrated, it would establish a threshold requirement for capital punishment to affect behavior, namely that "someone is seemingly listening." However, as detailed below, the committee concluded that no existing study has successfully made such a demonstration and that the obstacles to success for a future study are formidable. As importantly, the committee concluded that a successful demonstration would have limited informational value.

Studies of a single execution event are subject to the same problem that bedevils most before-after studies. Because the execution is not conducted in the context of a carefully controlled experimental setting, other factors that affect the homicide rate may coincide with the execution event. Some event studies attempt to deal with this problem by examining changes over very short periods of time, days or a week. Although shortening the time window of observation may provide some protection from the effects of other sources (but see discussion below), it opens other possible interpretations of the result. Even if a short-term effect could be established, it would be difficult to determine whether homicides were actually prevented or simply displaced in time. This possibility creates a fundamental conundrum: the study of short time frames increases the plausibility of the displacement in time interpretation, and the study of longer time frames increases the risk of confounding by other factors.

It is vital to understand that event studies do not speak to the question of whether and how a state's sanction regime affects its homicide rate. The simplest illustration of this point involves the interpretation of a study that fails to find evidence that an execution event affects the homicide rate. Consider, for example, a study of the first execution after an extended moratorium. Suppose that the study convincingly demonstrated that the execution was not followed by any change in the homicide rate. One interpretation of this result is that capital punishment has no deterrent effect. However, another possibility is that the deterrent effect is large but that it was anticipated in advance of the execution due to the publicity given to the upcoming event. Both possibilities are logical and plausible, but they are not distinguishable by the event study methodology.

Alternatively, suppose that an event study found that homicides are reduced in the immediate aftermath of an execution and not just displaced in time. To generalize from this single execution requires consideration of the context in which the execution occurred. If it was the first execution after an extended moratorium, it is problematic to assume that such an effect would recur for subsequent executions. More generally, the effect of any given execution may depend on the proximity in time of that execution to other executions and to the frequency of executions more generally. For example, if an execution event study established convincingly that it averted one homicide that week, it does not follow that each additional execution would avert one more homicide. To complicate matters further, the effect of any one execution may depend on the identity of the person executed (e.g., an infamous serial killer or a person for whom there is some public sympathy) and the amount of publicity given to the execution.

The problem of generalizing from the findings of even a convincing event study is indicative of still another fundamental committee concern with all the time-series studies. The researchers who carry out such studies never clearly specify why potential murderers respond to execution events. Do potential murderers respond to the shock value of execution? If so, would the magnitude of the shock value change with each additional execution? One possibility is that the shock value might increase, perhaps because of reinforcement. Alternatively, it might decrease, perhaps because a potential murderer becomes inured to executions. Still another possibility is that potential murderers respond to sanction risk probabilities and that execution events cause them to update their perceptions of those probabilities.

Studies of Deviations from Fitted Trends

This issue of why and how potential murderers react to executions is equally important to the interpretation of studies that combine data on executions and homicides over multiple time periods, deploying subtle time-series methods to analyze these data. Consider Figures 5-1 and 5-2, which plot executions and homicides, respectively, in Texas from 1990 to 2008. The most obvious way to examine the association of executions and homicides in Texas is to correlate these two time series. Over the period, this correlation is –0.68. However, there are innumerable obvious objections to interpreting this negative association as deterrence because many factors that influence the homicide rate were also changing over this time period. One manifestation of this observation can be seen in Figure 3-3 (in Chapter 3), which shows the close correspondence over time in the homi-

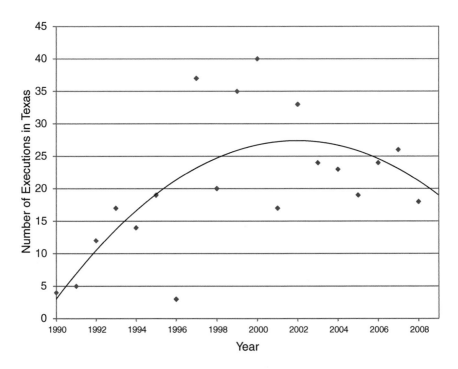

FIGURE 5-1 Executions in Texas from 1990 to 2008.
SOURCE: Data from Texas Department of Criminal Justice (2011).

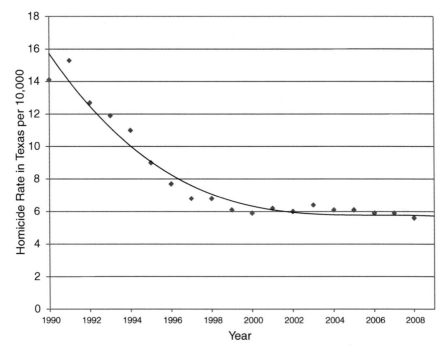

FIGURE 5-2 Texas homicide rate from 1990 to 2008.
SOURCES: Data from the Federal Bureau of Investigation (2011).

cide rates of three states with very different capital punishment sanction regimes—California, New York, and Texas.

Studies of executions and homicides over multiple time periods do not examine the raw time-series association between the homicide rate and number of executions. Instead they analyze the association between deviations from fitted statistical trend lines that summarize these two time series. One technical adjustment sometimes used to in these studies is that the data series be detrended. By "detrended" it is meant that the time series does not vary systematically with time (e.g., does not increase over time). As a consequence the time-series studies analyze the association between deviations from statistical trend lines that summarizes the execution time series and the homicide rate time series

As an illustration, consider again Figures 5-1 and 5-2. Superimposed on the raw time-series plots of executions and homicides are regression equations fit to the execution and homicide data. In the case of the execution time series, the regression uses a quadratic function of time to fit the raw data. In the case of the homicide time series, the regression uses a cubic function of time to fit the data.

The time-series literature views the fitted regressions as "trends" that should be subtracted from the raw data prior to analysis. After that subtraction, researchers analyze the statistical association between deviations from the respective trends to draw inferences about the effect of executions on homicides. For example, in 1998, during the peak period of executions in Texas, the deviation of the actual number of executions from the fitted trend line is negative. A time-series researcher might examine the statistical association between this negative deviation and corresponding deviations of the homicide rate from its fitted trend line in 1999 and later years.

Unfortunately, the researchers who carry out these studies do not explicitly state their rationale for analyzing deviations in this fashion. They may believe that this form of analysis provides a basis for causal interpretation of findings that is more credible than analysis of raw data on homicides and executions. However, the committee concludes that analysis of deviations from fitted trends, at least as conducted in the published studies, does not provide a valid basis for inferring the effects of executions on homicides.

One reason for our conclusion is that the study of deviations from fitted trend lines, even with high frequency data, may not avoid the confounding problem that affects analyses of the raw correlation of executions and homicide rates over time. For example, the publicity given to executions may still be systematically related to deviations from an execution trend line. Indeed, one of the studies we reviewed (Stolzenberg and D'Alessio, 2004) reports that, even in deviation form, the execution and publicity time series were highly correlated.

A more fundamental concern is that execution event studies do not clearly specify why potential murderers respond to execution events. For potential murderers to react to a deviation from a fitted trend line requires that they *recognize* it as a deviation. To recognize it as a deviation requires that they be aware of the trend line from which deviations are measured. However, none of the studies discusses why potential murderers might be attentive to the trend lines fit by time-series researchers and, if so, how they might react to deviations from fitted trends. Indeed, the studies do not even ask whether potential murderers perceive the time-series evidence on executions in terms of a trend and deviations from the trend.

If potential murderers are attentive to the trend line, there would have to be a reason for giving it their attention. One possibility is that their behavior is affected by the trend line. For example, the escalation of executions in Texas during the 1990s might have been interpreted as an intensification of the state's capital punishment sanction regime. Conventional deterrence theory would predict that such an escalation would reduce homicides, assuming that intensification of the use of capital punishment did not alter other aspects of the sanction regime. But the brutalization theory might predict that this escalation increases murders. Yet neither of these predictions speaks to the question of how potential murderers react to *deviations* from the trend.

Consider, for example, the conventional economic model of criminal decision making. This model assumes that potential murderers respond to their perceptions of the probability of capture and punishment, which in this context is execution. Under this model, unless potential murderers perceive a deviation from trend as signaling a change in the probability of execution, they will not change their behavior even though their behavior is affected by the probability of execution. Thus, from the perspective of the economic conception of deterrence, a finding of no association between deviations from fitted execution and homicide trends is not indicative of a lack of deterrence.

In making this point, it is important to emphasize that the committee is not endorsing this deterrence-based model of behavior. We pose it to illustrate that the results of time-series analyses are not interpretable in the absence of a behavioral model.

Another possible behavioral model might build from the assumption that potential murderers react in fear to the shock value of executions and are thereby dissuaded from committing a murder. This assumption, however, does not suffice to interpret the results of time-series analyses of deviations from fitted trends. Why should deviations from a fitted trend have shock value separate from the trend itself? If there is no apparent shock value to a deviation from the trend line, does that mean that the trend line itself has no shock value?

The idea that potential murderers perceive and react to deviations from fitted execution time trends presupposes that they are attentive to trends and have mental models of how trends are formed. Moreover, their perceptions of trends must coincide with those of the researchers who fit trend lines to raw execution data. Otherwise, potential murderers would have no basis for recognizing deviations as such.

If time-series analysis finds that homicide rates are responsive to such deviations, the question is why? One possibility is that potential murderers interpret a deviation as new information about the intensity of the application of capital punishment—that is, that the deviation signals a change in the part of the sanction regime that relates to the application of capital punishment. If so, a deviation from the execution trend line may cause potential murderers to alter their perceptions of the future course of the trend line, which in turn may change their behavior.

Yet, even accepting this idea, a basic question persists. Why should the trend lines fit by researchers coincide with the perceptions of potential murderers about trends in executions? If researchers and potential murderers do not perceive trends the same way, then time-series analyses do not correctly identify what potential murderers perceive as deviations. However, the published time-series studies do not ask whether and how potential murderers perceive trends. Moreover, no study performs an empirical analysis that tries to learn how potential murderers perceive the risk of sanctions. Hence, the committee has no basis for assessing whether the findings of time-series studies reflect a real effect of executions on homicides or are artifacts of models that incorrectly specify how deviations cause potential murderers to update their forecasts of the future course of executions.

VECTOR AUTOREGRESSIONS

Evidence Under Existing Criminal Sanction Regimes

One methodology used in time-series studies of deterrence is known as vector autoregressions (VARs). Research of this type estimates dynamic regressions that relate current homicide and execution rates to previous realizations of these two variables. The estimated relationships are then used to make inference about deterrence. Although this methodology has only recently been applied in studies of capital punishment and deterrence, it has been long used in studies of imprisonment and crime: see Durlauf and Nagin (2011) for a review. We extensively discuss its limitations as a source of information on deterrence because it is the methodological state of the art in time-series approaches to deterrence, and it seems poised to become widespread in capital punishment studies, despite the shortcomings we discuss.

VARs were originally developed by macroeconometricians to describe the time-series evolution of an economy (Granger, 1969; Sims, 1972, 1980; Sims, Goldfeld, and Sachs, 1982). The methodology was motivated by the idea that the evolution of an economy can usefully be represented as the superposition of short-run cyclical fluctuations on long-run trends. This idea suggests a three-step analysis. One first uses the raw time-series data on the economy to estimate the trends. One then "detrends" the raw data by subtracting the estimated trends. The detrending step also subtracts the means of each variable, to produce residuals that have no trend and zero mean. One finally estimates a VAR on the detrended and "demeaned" residual data to study the time-series properties of the short-run fluctuations.

VARs are commonly specified to be linear regressions. The use of linear regression is motivated by a statistical idea rather than a substantive one. That is, under relatively weak technical conditions, any stationary time-series can be represented as a dynamic linear relationship that is recoverable from observation of the series.[1] The detrending step of the VAR methodology is intended to render the residual time series stationary.

Some criminologists have used VARs to study deterrence. An immediate question is whether it makes sense to think of the time-series evolution of homicides and executions as the superposition of short-run cyclical fluctuations on long-run trends. The researchers have used various definitions of trends, assuming them to be either linear or nonlinear functions of time. The absence of a consensus approach to detrending reflects the absence of any persuasive theory of the generation of the purported trends. In any case, after detrending is somehow accomplished, VARs are estimated on the detrended residual data and used to describe short-run cyclical fluctuations in homicides and executions.

To illustrate the methodology, denote the detrended and demeaned homicide and execution rates in political unit i at time t as $h_{i,t}$ and $e_{i,t}$, respectively, and suppose that there are multiple observations on these variables over time.[2] The VAR representation of these rates is a two equation system of linear regressions

$$h_{i,t} = a_1 h_{i,t-1} + a_2 h_{i,t-2} + \ldots + b_1 e_{i,t-1} + b_2 e_{i,t-2} + \ldots + \varepsilon_{i,t}$$
$$e_{i,t} = c_1 h_{i,t-1} + c_2 h_{i,t-2} + \ldots + d_1 e_{i,t-1} + d_2 e_{i,t-2} + \ldots + \eta_{i,t} \qquad (5\text{-}1)$$

Thus, a VAR linearly relates current executions and homicides to previous executions and homicides, as well as to the current values of the random variables $\varepsilon_{i,t}$ and $\eta_{i,t}$. The choice of how many lagged terms to use is made with the intention that $\varepsilon_{i,t}$ and $\eta_{i,t}$ be random variables that are uncorrelated across time. That is, these two random variables may be correlated at a point in time, but future and previous values cannot be correlated. Formally, $\varepsilon_{i,t}$ and $\eta_{i,t}$ are the one-period-ahead prediction errors for homicides and executions given that predictor variables are restricted to the linear histories of these variables.[3] In the relatively simple case in which only finite lags appear in (1), the coefficients of the VAR may be estimated by ordinary least squares.

In studies of the deterrent effect of capital punishment, systems such as (5-1) have focused on the coefficients $b_1, b_2,\ldots$, which relate lagged levels of execution rates to the time t homicide rate. If the b_i coefficients are all equal to 0, then execution rates are said *not* to "Granger-cause" homicide rates. That term comes from econometrician Clive Granger, who proposed

---

[1]This is known as the autoregression form of the Wold representation theorem: see Ash and Gardner (1975) for a fully rigorous treatment.

[2]Some studies use levels rather than rates, but this distinction is not essential for understanding the methodology.

[3]By linear, we refer to the fact that prediction of homicides and executions are not allowed to depend on more complicated functions of their joint histories than the additive structure in (1).

this statistical definition of causality as a way to summarize the dynamic relationships between time series. It is essential to understand that use of the word "cause" notwithstanding, a finding that the b_1 coefficients are all equal to 0 is only a statement about the absence of a linear statistical relationship between current homicides and lagged executions, conditioning on lagged homicides. It is not a statement about causality as it is commonly understood in social science research that distinguishes statistical association from causation. The absence of Granger causality from execution rates to homicide rates only means that the best linear prediction of homicide rates, given the joint histories of homicide and execution rates, does not require knowledge of the history of execution rates; the history of homicides rates is sufficient. The absence of Granger causality does not imply that a counterfactual change in executions because of a change in the sanction regime facing potential murderers would fail to generate changes in homicides at later dates.

Despite the fact that Granger causality is only a statistical concept, findings on the statistical question of whether executions Granger-cause homicides have been used to make substantive claims about the deterrent effect of capital punishment. The absence of Granger causality has been interpreted by some researchers as evidence that capital punishment does not have a deterrent effect on homicides. In studies in which the estimates of the b_i coefficients are negative, such findings have been alleged to be evidence of a deterrent effect, with higher execution rates in the past generating lower homicide rates in the future. In studies in which estimates of the b_i coefficients are positive, those findings have been alleged to be evidence of a brutalization effect, with higher execution rates in the past generating higher homicide rates in the future.

In a study of the time-series relationships between homicides and executions, as well as the relationship between homicides and execution publicity in Houston, Stolzenberg and D'Alessio (2004) use this approach. The authors find that neither actual executions nor publicity about executions Granger-cause homicides and conclude that neither deterrence nor brutalization effects are present in the Houston data.

Land, Teske, and Zhang (2009) provide a particularly sophisticated analysis of this type, using data from Texas, by focusing directly on how a one-unit increase in $\eta_{i,t}$ affects homicides at $t + 1$, $t + 2$, etc. In order to render this a well-posed question, it is necessary to address the contemporaneous correlation between $\eta_{i,t}$, the one-step-ahead prediction error to executions, and $\varepsilon_{i,t}$ the one-step-ahead prediction error to homicides. In essence, Land, Teske, and Zhang resolve this contemporaneous correlation by assuming that $\varepsilon_{i,t} = \rho \eta_{i,t} + v_{i,t}$ such that $\varepsilon_{i,t}$ and $v_{i,t}$ are contemporaneously uncorrelated, and so treat $v_{i,t}$ as the shock to homicides. Thus, the contemporaneous correlation between $\eta_{i,t}$ and $\varepsilon_{i,t}$ is resolved by assuming that the shock to homicides is due to the shock to executions and some other unspecified factor. The researchers do not provide a model of the timing of executions, so it is difficult to assess this assumption.[4] They find a negative association between executions and homicide and conclude that there is a net small deterrent effect from an additional execution. However, they also find that executions appear to displace homicides in time. Thus, the long-run deterrent effect is smaller than the short-run effect.

Taken on their own terms, Stolzenberg and D'Alessio (2004) and Land, Teske, and Zhang (2009) provide contradictory evidence on deterrence. Even though each paper uses monthly data from Texas, the papers reach opposite conclusions about the evidence of a deterrent effect. This does not mean that either paper contains errors, as the data sets used and the choice of VAR specification differ across the papers. Nonetheless, the papers' contradictory findings illustrate that conclusions about a deterrent effect can be very sensitive to the choice of model and details as to how data are transformed prior to estimation. What might be thought to be relatively innocuous assumptions can matter greatly.

This observation leads to a broader critique of both papers. Neither asks what conclusions about deterrence can be drawn when one does not assume a particular time-series specification or when one allows for different deterrent effects in different time periods. Neither the time-series specification nor the appropriate data range are known a priori to a researcher. Although both papers engage in model selection exercises in order to generate specific VAR forms, this approach is inadequate for policy purposes. Model selection methods in essence assign a weight of 1 to the "best" model, given some criterion, but the data themselves do not necessarily assign such a weight. In other words, neither paper appropriately accounts for model uncertainty in providing deterrence estimates. The committee returns to this issue in Chapter 6.

A more basic question is whether evidence of the type presented in the Land, Teske, and Zhang (2009) and Stolzenberg and D'Alessio (2004) analyses actually speaks to the question of the deterrent effect of capital punishment. VARs only measure statistical associations in data. Thus, the fundamental question is the relationship between the statistical concept of Granger causality and the policy-relevant concept of causality as treatment response. The remainder of this section mainly discusses this basic issue. We then raise a second concern about criminological research that uses VARs.

---

[4]One might plausibly argue that the assumption holds when time increments are short. However it may be that the judicial system's willingness to grant stays of execution is affected by recent homicide activity, particularly when the homicides generate publicity.

Granger Causality and Causality as Treatment Response

The idea that Granger causality speaks to a deterrent effect of capital punishment is not a logical implication of social science theory. There may perhaps be theories of deterrence in which the presence of a deterrence effect would be equivalent to the statistical concept of Granger causality, but no such theory has yet been advanced. However, there already exist standard models of criminal behavior under which Granger causality tests are uninformative about deterrence.

For the sake of concreteness, we focus on the model of rational criminal behavior that has been the workhorse of much of the modern theory of deterrence, that of Becker (1968). This model, which assumes that the choice of whether to commit a crime (in this case, homicide) can be understood as a purposeful choice in which costs and benefits are compared, is controversial among some criminologists, sociologists, and economists. A particular concern has been the common assumption that potential criminals not only behave rationally, but also have so-called rational expectations; that is, that they correctly perceive the sanctions risk that they face. The discussion below should not be interpreted as a committee endorsement of this specific assumption or of the idea of rational criminal behavior more broadly. The discussion is meant to illustrate how this widely used theoretical formulation sharply delimits what can be learned from standard VAR estimates.

Put simply, the rational-criminal model places *no* restrictions on the presence or absence of Granger causality from executions to homicides. The reason the model does not imply such time-series restrictions on the relationship between executions and homicides is not a function of its specific rationality assumptions; rather, the central point is that the rational-criminal model supposes that individual beliefs about sanctions risks derive from their perception of the criminal sanction regime in which they live, not from the occurrence of executions per se.

The idea of a sanction regime is that a potential murderer faces a probability distribution of outcomes that will stem from the choice of committing murder. The first uncertain outcome is whether the murderer will be caught. Conditional on being caught, the potential murderer then faces a probability distribution of punishments. With some simplification of the way the criminal justice system works, the beliefs of a potential murderer about three probabilities matter: (1) the probability of not being caught, P_{NC}, (2) the probability of being caught and serving a prison sentence, P_P,[5] and (3) the probability of being caught and being executed, P_E. It is standard to regard $P_C = 1 - P_{NC}$ as the certainty of punishment. The outcomes of imprisonment and execu-

---

[5]In this example, we assume that there is a single prison sentence length for murder. In practice, there are many potential prison sentence lengths and a rational criminal will account for the probabilities of each of the sentences.

tion constitute the severity of punishment. The criminal sanction regime is defined by those probabilities and the two outcomes, sentence length if not executed and execution.

From the vantage of the rational-criminal model, short-run fluctuations in the occurrence of executions are *irrelevant* to murder decisions unless they cause individuals to revise their beliefs about the certainty and severity of punishment if a murder is committed. Although one can construct theories as to why the occurrence of executions would lead to revisions in beliefs (and one can find examples of such theories in the literature), tests of Granger causality as they have so far been used do not speak to the deterrence question. In particular, they ignore the distinction between the criminal sanction regime and the time-series realizations of one of the potential punishments under that regime, namely, executions. We emphasize that this point does not depend on the assumption that potential murderers rationally weigh the costs and benefits of murder. Rather, it rests on the much weaker assumption that potential murderers respond to their beliefs about sanction risks and not about execution events per se.

More specifically, a potential murderer makes the decision to commit a homicide against the background of a set of uncertain outcomes to that act. In a rational-criminal model, beliefs about sanction risk are not necessarily affected by the occurrence of a relatively high or low number of executions during the previous month or during any other time period. A potential murderer may simply interpret time-series fluctuations in the occurrence of executions as a reflection of time-series fluctuations in the number of people convicted of murder several years earlier, each execution taking place under a stationary sanction regime. Thus, execution events themselves need not alter perceptions of the sanction regime. It follows that an empirical finding of no Granger causality does not necessarily imply the absence of a deterrence effect to capital punishment.

Furthermore, if the candidate explanations for criminal behavior are either that criminals are not subject to deterrent effects or that potential murderers obey a rational model of criminal behavior, then Granger causality from executions to homicides does not necessarily provide support for the deterrence explanation. For example, suppose the rational choice theory of deterrence, which does not embody any explanation of the timing of executions, is correct. For the rational choice models under a stable sanction regime, Granger causality from fluctuations in executions to fluctuations in homicides tautologically occurs because of factors outside of changes in the sanction regime. Hence, Granger causality from executions to homicides cannot be attributed to the deterrence mechanism of the rational choice model. The upshot is that the validity of the claim of deterrence cannot alone be assessed by either the presence or the absence of Granger causality from executions to homicides. It must be assessed in the context of a behavioral model whether of the rational choice variety or not.

Under the rational-criminal model, one can potentially connect execution events to behavior if one discards the specific assumption of rational expectations and instead supposes that people use data on the occurrence of executions to update their subjective beliefs about the sanction regime in which they live. Suggestions of such updating appear in the some studies, but the committee is unaware of any formal model of beliefs and behavior that make tests of Granger causality that have interpretable implications for deterrence. Furthermore, as we emphasized earlier in the report, remarkably little is known about the perceptions of would-be murderers or about how their perceptions may change in response to executions.

Choice of Variables in VAR Studies

The use of vector autoregressions in the empirical studies of capital punishment and deterrence suffers from a second important limitation: insufficient attention to the choice of variables in the systems under study. The studies that use Granger causality to study deterrence have been almost exclusively focused on bivariate relations of the type described by equation (5-1). Although bivariate systems are relatively straightforward to analyze, especially when one is interested in the effects of shocks to one series on the behavior of another, they are not nearly as sophisticated as the form of vector autoregression analysis that is now conventionally used in macroeconomics, the field from which these methods are taken. In fact, the evolution of atheoretical models in macroeconomics has illustrated the importance of thinking about the time-series relationships among different collections of variables. Modern vector autoregression analysis works with far more complex systems than the bivariate ones found in studies of capital punishment.[6]

Without carefully specifying the set of relevant variables, findings from the VAR studies on deterrence and capital punishment may be an artifice of the choice of executions as the only variable that can affect homicides. For capital punishment, there is an obvious lacuna when focus is restricted to executions and homicides: entirely omitted are variables that measure the severity of punishment for murderers who are not executed. Virtually any behaviorally plausible formulation of deterrence would suggest that these variables are an essential part of the sanction regime relevant to a would-be murderer's behavior.

The omission of time series of data that describe the noncapital pun-

---

[6]For example, Leeper, Sims, and Zha (1996) analyze systems that use 13 and 18 distinct variables to study monetary policy and draw explicit contrasts with more parsimonious systems.

ishments meted out for homicides means that the bivariate systems omit critical variables necessary for complete description of a sanction regime. Therefore, even if people use observations of realized fluctuations in punishments to update their perceptions of sanction regimes, bivariate models cannot be interpreted as giving evidence of the deterrent effect of capital punishment per se. Fluctuations in the occurrence of executions may be correlated with fluctuations in the severity of the prison terms received by murderers who do not receive the death penalty, generating a classic problem of omitted variables. The omitted variables problem affects vector autoregressions just as it affects other types of regressions: spurious correlations may be produced and parameter estimates may be biased.

This argument can be generalized. Crime rates are well understood to vary with a host of demographic and socioeconomic variables. Land, Teske, and Zhang (2009) and Stolzenberg and D'Alessio (2004) omit such variables from their analyses. Findings of Granger causality or its absence depends on the set of variables under consideration. Therefore, by the standards of the modern use of vector autoregressions, neither of these studies considers a rich enough system of variables to justify interpreting their findings in terms of deterrence.

Inferences Under Alternative Sanction Regimes

The discussion above has concerned inference on deterrence under existing sanction regimes. A distinct question concerns the capacity of atheoretical time-series methods in general and Granger causality tests in particular to provide information on the deterrent effect of capital punishment under alternative sanction regimes from those that have existed and currently exist in the United States. As described elsewhere in this report, the historical capital punishment regime is one in which executions are very infrequent in comparison with the numbers of homicides. Furthermore, when a murderer is apprehended, execution typically does not occur even when the murderer receives the death penalty in trial. Liebman, Fagan, and West (2000) found that two-thirds of capital sentences are reversed on appeal. As we note elsewhere in the report, only 15 percent of capital sentences meted out between 1973 and 2009 have ended in an actual execution.

The alleged strength of atheoretical time-series methods—which is evinced in their reliance on the properties of the historical data as opposed to a priori assumptions on how people or groups behave—has the necessary consequence that these methods cannot speak to the deterrent effects of substantively different criminal sanction regimes. Alternative criminal sanction regimes would imply different coefficients for the vector autoregression system (5-1) if the individuals' decision making or the process generating executions was different under an alternative regime. In other words, the relationship between homicides and executions may depend on the criminal sanction regime. Hence, the historical relationships that are estimated when a system such as (5-1) is applied to data may change with the regime.

In macroeconomics, this dependence of statistical relationships on the underlying policy regime (in this case, the sanction regime for murder) is known as the Lucas critique (Lucas, 1976), although the idea goes back to Marschak (1953). In the case of capital punishment, the force of the Lucas-Marschak critique is self-evident. The available data on executions and homicides are generated in a context in which actual executions are quite unusual. As such, they are unlikely to provide useful information on hypothetical regimes under which capital sentences are regularly carried out.[7]

EVENT STUDIES

A second time-series approach used to study deterrence is what we will call the "event study" because it focuses on the association between homicide and a single execution or particular executions. This work takes seriously the idea that an execution is an unusual event and implicitly assumes that the event is of sufficient importance, considered relative to the background of other determinants of homicide, that it leaves a discernible footprint in the homicide time series.

This type of analysis was first performed by Phillips (1980), who identified 22 executions of "notorious murderers" in England in the period 1858-1921. For each execution, he studied the number of homicides in London in the weeks before and after the execution. He found a statistically significant difference between homicide rates in the week prior to an execution and the week after an execution. A more detailed analysis found that this reduction was subsequently reversed, so that homicides were displaced in time rather than reduced. In light of these results, Zeisel (1982) argued that Phillips' evidence should be thought of as a delay rather than a deterrent effect. Phillips (1982) did not dispute this alternative interpretation in his rejoinder.

In our view, the Phillips study is not useful in assessing deterrence effects. One issue, raised by Zeisel, is that the narrow time horizon studied before and after the executions makes it hard to distinguish displacement from deterrence. Another serious problem is Phillips' assumption that in the absence of a deterrent effect of execution, the process generating homicides

---

[7]This distinction is well understood in the macroeconomic literature using vector autoregressions. Leeper and Zha (2003), for example, explicitly define criteria for "modest" policy interventions under which VARs may be used for policy evaluation. The explicit objective of their work is to identify vectors of shocks that occur with high enough probability that their effects may be evaluated under the assumption that the policy regime generating the shocks is unchanged.

is stationary over time. This assumption motivates his test of the null hypothesis that the homicide rate in the week before an execution is the same as in the week after it. There is little reason to believe this null hypothesis given that there are many potential sources of time variation in the determinants of homicides beyond the effects of executions. As a stark example of how Phillips' approach can lead to spurious inferences, suppose that England experienced a long-run decline in homicide during the 1858-1921 period that Phillips studied. In that situation, the data would tend to show lower homicide rates in the week after executions than in the week before simply because the week after occurs later than the week before. Without a full specification of the properties of the total homicide process, one cannot understand the effects of individual executions.

Another limitation of Phillips' analysis concerns external validity. It is not clear that the homicide process for England in 1858-1921 is the same as that for the modern United States. By analogy, one would not use data on the effects of changes in fiscal policy from 1858-1921 to evaluate current macroeconomic policy proposals.

A second example of this style of analysis is Cochran, Chamblin, and Seth (1994), which analyzed the effects of a particular execution on homicides in Oklahoma. The execution studied was that of Charles Troy Coleman. Coleman's execution was the first in Oklahoma in 25 years. In addition to sharing the same limitations as those in Phillips' study, the Oklahoma study has a fatal flaw in the research design. To see this, we describe some of the details of the model used.

The raw data for the study were weekly homicides in Oklahoma, which we denote as $H_{OK,t}$. Prior to their analysis, the authors detrended and demeaned this time series. The researchers next regressed the residuals on lagged residuals. The result was a white-noise data series, $\varepsilon_{OK,t}$ which represents the one-step-ahead forecast errors when $H_{OK,t}$ is regressed against its history, after any constant term and trends are removed. They then defined an intervention time series, I_t, which equals 0 prior to the execution and 1 afterward. Finally, they estimated the equation

$$\varepsilon_{OK,t} = \alpha_0 I_t + \alpha_1 I_{t-1} + \ldots + \xi_{OK,t} \qquad (5\text{-}2)$$

where $\xi_{OK,t}$ is a prediction error. They interpreted the coefficient α_1 as measuring the effects of the execution. Different restrictions on this coefficient were considered. For example, if the α_1 is required to sum to 0, this imposes the restriction that there can be no permanent effect of the execution on homicide rates, only a displacement effect.

The key conceptual problem with this approach is that it is logically impossible for a white-noise stochastic process to be correlated with an intervention series as it is defined here—there may be a correlation in a finite data sample but not in the population. The reason is simple: the white-noise series has a mean of 0 and the intervention series does not. Hence, there is *nothing* that can be learned from the exercise involving specifications that do not impose the restriction that the long-run effect of the execution on homicides is zero. In terms of the underlying time-series mathematics, the "pre-whitening" described in the study assumes statistical properties for the homicide series that are inconsistent with equation 5-2 (see Charles and Durlauf, in press, for details). The authors argue the best specification for 5-2 is one that does not impose the requirement that the α_1 coefficient sums to 0. In other words, the authors argue that the best specification for the effect of an execution on homicides is one that cannot in a population produce the result they assert holds in the finite sample.

A more persuasive example of an event study of deterrence is Hjalmarsson (2009). Methodologically, the approach in this paper originated in Grogger (1990), who proposed an appropriate statistical model for such an analysis, treating the homicide level as a count variable. We focus on the Hjalmarsson paper because it uses daily data and specifically focus on cities in which capital punishment is relatively common.

The analysis considered very short-run effects of executions in Dallas, Houston, and San Antonio, Texas. For the study, the daily counts of homicides in the cities were analyzed to see whether homicide rates varied in the days before and after an execution. Hjalmarsson found little evidence of a "local" (in time) deterrence effect. She was careful not to extrapolate her results to broader concepts of deterrence, recognizing that her limited time horizon does not allow one to distinguish between displacement and deterrence. As such, the analysis suffers from one of the same flaws as Phillips (1980), but her use of daily homicide counts may be useful to discern the immediate visceral effect of an execution.

We caution, however, that even this extremely short-run analysis may be susceptible to the problem that events relevant to homicide may co-occur with executions. To give one simple example, police departments may alter deployments of personnel in the periods immediately following executions that draw public attention. If so, one cannot interpret fluctuations in homicides immediately before and after an execution in terms of the deterrent effect of the execution.

TIME-SERIES REGRESSIONS

Another strand of the literature estimates time-series regressions that relate homicide rates or levels to executions and other covariates. Although VARs are also time-series regressions, the work discussed in this section differs in several respects from the work discussed above. First, the regressions are estimated using raw homicide and execution data rather than detrended and demeaned data. Second, lagged homicides are not included among the variables used to predict current homicides. Third, various other covariates than lags of executions and homicides are used among the predictor variables.

One example is the study by Bailey (1998), which considered the Coleman execution in Oklahoma, but it modifies some aspects of Cochran, Chamblin, and Seth (1994). In particular, this paper works with the time series of the level of homicides rather than a transformation of the time series into a white noise process, and it further includes various predictor variables in addition to the event of the execution to model the homicide level. Unfortunately, the paper does not report any equations, but the description it provides suggests that the analysis is based on the regression

$$H_{OK,t} = \kappa + \alpha I_t + \beta_0 E_{US,t} + \beta_1 E_{US,t-1}$$
$$+ \ldots \gamma_0 P_{OK,t} + \gamma_1 P_{OK,t-1} + \ldots + \delta X_t + \varepsilon_t \tag{5-3}$$

In this regression, $E_{US,t}$ is a measure of the number of executions in the United States. The idea is that the public may be aware of these executions through various channels. $P_{OK,t}$ is a measure of the publicity given to executions throughout the country, as measured by days of newspaper coverage in the *Oklahoman* in a given week. This variable is intended to measure public information about executions; it is distinct from $E_{US,t}$ in that it measures a particular information source. X_t is a vector of control variables, which include socioeconomic and demographic characteristics, as well as month-specific dummy variables; these dummies are included for ad hoc reasons. The study finds that the overall level of murders is positively associated with the publicity variables. When focus is limited to overall killings of strangers, as well as subsets of this category, the results are mixed, with some regressions finding a brutalization effect, others finding no effect, and some cases finding a deterrence effect.

Despite these mixed results, Bailey concludes that "No prior study has shown such strong support for the capital punishment and brutalization argument" (Bailey, 1998, p. 711). The author, in our view, overstates his findings by focusing on regressions with statistically significant coefficients. Other regressions, in which statistical significance fails, are not accounted for in the author's strong conclusions. As noted in Chapter 4, a finding that an estimate is statistically insignificant does not imply that the true deterrent effect is zero or even that it is small. In other words, the study does not properly account for the dependence of the brutalization findings on particular regression specifications.

Beyond the specifics of Bailey's study, this type of regression analysis, although still common in the social sciences, does not support causal claims. Regressions of this type are based on many arbitrary assumptions, such as linearity of the effects of executions and other variables on homicides, as well as particular choice of control variables, without attention to the effects of alternative choices. Furthermore, despite the author's claims, the execution of Coleman does not constitute a quasi-experiment. The timing of the execution is likely to be an endogenous outcome of the criminal justice system and should be modeled as such.

A different type of time-series regression analysis has been used by Cloninger (1992) and Cloninger and Marchesini (2001, 2006). These papers in essence estimate time-series regressions of the form

$$\Delta H_{i,t} = \kappa + \beta \Delta H_{US,t} + \varepsilon_{i,t} \qquad (5\text{-}4)$$

Here $\Delta H_{i,t}$ denotes the change across years in the homicide rate in place I, and $\Delta H_{US,t}$ denotes the similar change in the United States as a whole. The researchers attempt to motivate this regression specification by analogy to the capital asset pricing model (CAPM) of finance.[8] These studies, for periods with executions, evaluate deterrence by asking whether β, the average of $\Delta H_{i,t}$, and the average of $\varepsilon_{i,t}$ is smaller in periods in which capital punishment either is possible or actually occurs. Taken as a whole, these studies find a deterrent effect for a capital punishment regime.

The committee concludes that the findings of these studies are not interpretable as providing evidence of a deterrent effect. The basic problem is that the analogy between a portfolio of assets and a portfolio of crimes is specious. The homicide model under study is constructed exclusively by analogy with finance. It pays no attention to the criminal justice system as an input in criminal decisions, time constraints on the part of criminals, differences in the reasons for crimes, etc. The various studies that use this methodology assert that all such factors are incorporated in the coefficient β, but there is no reason to believe that this is true. Because CAPM is predicated on investors' optimally investing in financial instruments in the context of competitive markets for these products, for Cloninger's specification to be sensible he would have to demonstrate that potential murderers engage in an analogous optimization problem that is aggregated to produce state-level homicide rates. No attempt is made to demonstrate this analogy.

CROSS-POLITY COMPARISONS

Yet another time-series approach to measuring the deterrent effect of capital punishment is comparison of time series for homicides in two countries, one of which has capital punishment and the other of which does not,

---

[8]The capital asset pricing model describes the relationship between risk and expected return for different assets. See Brennan (2008) for a description.

to see whether one can identify differences between the time series that may be plausibly attributed to capital punishment. In Chapter 3, for example, the committee displays homicide rates in, California, New York, and Texas, from 1974 through the early 1990s (see Figure 3-3) to illustrate the importance of accounting for variations, across time and place, in factors that influence murder rates other than the use of capital punishment. Donohue and Wolfers (2005) use this method and argue that the close tracking of the U.S. and Canadian homicide rates calls into question any deterrence effect to the death penalty, since this punishment only exists in the United States. Their argument is at best suggestive because they do not account for common trends in the two series, let alone common factors, such as the interdependence of the Canadian and American economies. It also does not take into account the de facto moratorium in the death penalty in the United States prior to the *Furman* decision. Thus, the fact that the U.S. and Canadian homicide series are highly correlated is not a legitimate basis for concluding that there is no deterrent effect of capital punishment in the United States.

In examining the cross-country differences in the homicide series in Singapore and Hong Kong, Zimring, Fagan, and Johnson (2010), to their credit, recognized that an informal comparison from two selected entities alone is not sufficient to draw inferences. Unfortunately, their more systematic efforts cannot address the data and modeling flaws in the study.

The basic idea of the Zimring, Fagan, and Johnson (2010) study is to see whether differences in the Singapore and Hong Kong homicide rates can be explained by execution rates in Singapore, none having occurred in Hong Kong over the time frame of the analysis. Letting $h_{S,t}$ denote the Singapore homicide rate in year t and $h_{HK,t}$ the Hong Kong homicide rate in year t, the paper examines whether $h_{S,t} - h_{HK,t}$, once trends are accounted for, is associated with either the execution rate for Singapore or the execution level in Singapore. Both contemporaneous and lagged effects of these execution variables are considered.

Singapore and Hong Kong were chosen on the basis that they are very similar polities, so that differences in the homicide rates between them cannot be attributed to differences in demographics or socioeconomic factors. The researchers further argue that the relative commonality of executions in Singapore in contrast with the United States makes the analysis of the two cities particularly informative. The study concludes that executions do not have predictive power for homicide differences between the two cities.

The committee concludes that this study fails to provide evidence on the deterrence question. One problem with the analysis has already been raised in our critical discussion above of the vector autoregression approach to deterrence: the failure to distinguish between the effects of a sanction regime on homicides and the effects of fluctuations in the rate of executions. The researchers argue that "Singapore is a best case for deterrence because a death sentence is mandatory for murder and because of celerity in the appeals process" (Zimring, Fagan, and Johnson, 2010, p. 2). In other words, Singapore, like Hong Kong, has a constant sanction regime over the sample. The authors (pp. 9-10) raise the idea that the execution rate matters for a potential murderer's beliefs about the likelihood of being executed, but this assertion is rendered less plausible by their claims of regime stability for Singapore. If one thinks that deterrence depends on perceptions of the sanction regime, then the authors' own argument about regime stability undermines a role for executions in learning. Such stability eliminates one channel by which executions might be informative about deterrence.

A distinct reason that this study is not informative about the deterrent effect of capital punishment is that the key assumption underlying the analysis—that any systematic or predictable component of the homicide rate difference, $h_{HK,t} - h_{S,t}$, can only be due to capital punishment—is not credible. The paper's own regressions lead inevitably to this conclusion. In addition to studying the difference $h_{HK,t} - h_{S,t}$, the researchers also perform regressions of the Singapore homicide rate $h_{S,t}$ on the Hong Kong homicide rate $h_{HK,t}$ and their various execution measures. The logic of their thought experiment would require that $h_{HK,t}$ is a statistically significant predictor of $h_{S,t}$, with a regression coefficient of 1. The validity of their analysis, in other words, is predicated on the assumption that the homicide rate in Hong Kong is a sufficient statistic for the homicide rate in Singapore, except for the presence of capital punishment in Singapore. In fact, the study found that the homicide rate in Hong Kong fails to predict the homicide rate in Singapore: the coefficient is far from 1 in value and far from statistical significance. Hence, the researchers' own analysis indicates that the key assumption that justifies their analysis is not valid.

The study by Zimring, Fagan, and Johnson (2009) also suffers from first-order data problems. As the researchers note, the government of Singapore does not publish statistics on executions, and it routinely executes individuals convicted of a wide variety of crimes other than homicide. This leads the researchers to rely on constructed measures of executions and executions for murder. However, there are problems in the use of these constructed series. First, measurement error in independent variables produces biased estimates of coefficients; in the standard bivariate regression model, this bias reduces coefficient magnitude toward 0. Hence, their finding of a lack of evidence may be due to defects in their measure. The best the researchers can say about their estimated overall homicide series is that "we have developed a reliable minimum estimate of Singapore executions since 1981" (Zimring, Fagan, and Johnson, 2009, p. 7). This is uninformative as to what the degree of bias is in their estimates.

Second, the authors end up in an incoherent position in terms of mapping executions to the perceptions of potential murderers. In response to the lack of data on the split between executions for murder and executions for other crime, they argue that "But, of course, no data are available to the citizens of Singapore either, so the gross execution rate may be the appropriate risk for homicide to the extent that potential homicide offenders are aware of executions" (p. 6). The authors give no explanation as to how the potential murderers could possibly be aware of the overall execution rate but have no knowledge of the execution rate for particular offenses. Since the researchers conclude that data limitations prevent them from providing "stable and robust estimates of the unique effects of murder executions on murder" (p. 22), it is not clear why their negative findings on deterrence are informative about deterrence for murder.

The issue is not whether the authors did the best they could with the limited data, but whether the limited data allow one to draw inferences about deterrence. Note as well that given the researchers' own description of capital punishment in Singapore—"The secret nature of both individual executions and aggregate murder statistics must be a deliberate choice of the highly centralized and statistically meticulous Singapore government" (p. 10)—there is no good reason to believe that any results from their study are informative about capital punishment in the United States, where information available to the public is of course completely different, leaving aside all other differences between the two countries.

CONCLUSIONS

The committee analysis of the different strategies for using time series to uncover deterrent effects for capital punishment has consistently found the inferential claims to be flawed, whether the study in question does or does not find evidence of a deterrence effect. A common theme in our critiques of individual studies is that the underlying "decision theory" of potential murderers is consistently un- or underspecified, so that the implications of the time-series relationships between executions and homicide rates is unclear. Why should actual executions, as opposed to the sanction regime, matter? As discussed above, following the logic of the strong form of the rational-criminal model that assumes rational expectations, there should be no effect from executions by themselves, since the sanction regime entirely determines the deterrence effect. This fact means that the time-series studies suffer from a common identification problem: the existence of plausible theories of the behavior of potential murderers for which the time-series relationships are uninformative about the presence or absence of a deterrence effect, let alone its magnitude.

Of course, it is possible that the correct behavioral model for potential murderers is one for which the time-series relationships are informative.

One possibility is that actual executions affect a potential murderer's subjective probability of being executed if he commits the crime. If this is the rationale for the exercises, then Texas is not the ideal context for a study because executions are sufficiently routine in Texas that one would expect the informational content of a specific occurrence to be low. Yet because of the state's high fraction of executions nationally, Texas data are frequently used for studies. Texas might have experienced changes in the execution sanction regime, which would be useful for identifying deterrent effects, but this perspective has not been systematically explored, despite some occasional references to regime shifts in Texas.[9] In this respect, we think that the focus on Texas in the time-series literature may be misguided.

Another behavioral framework under which these exercises are informative is one in which an execution renders the possibility of the punishment more salient to a potential murderer. But such a framework would appear to imply that the effects of an execution will exhibit heterogeneity across types of potential murderers. For example, when murder is a crime of passion, one might argue that executive mental functioning is impaired. Hence, in this case salience comes into play because of a diminished capacity in thinking about consequences. Alternatively, one could argue that the impairment is such that the consequences of the action do not affect choice. This example illustrates that the implications of salience claims are far from obvious. Furthermore, we are unaware of any work that directly addresses salience as a source of deterrence and does so in a way that respects the fact that one needs a model of behavior, whether of the rational choice type or not, to interpret statistical findings.

Finally, we note that it is not even clear that executions per se are the source of salience. Is it obvious that actual executions are the main source of salience of the death penalty rather than, say, highly publicized death sentences? How do changes in the law or Supreme Court decisions affect salience? In the committee's search of relevant studies, we did not find any in which the sources of salience were explored. Hence, although it is a perfectly logically coherent idea that executions make capital punishment salient and provides a deterrence effect for this reason, there is no empirical work to justify the claim. One of the recommendations in Chapter 6 will involve the collection of data on perceptions of sanction regime, which would facilitate such empirical work.

Another distinct problem with the time-series studies is that they do

---

[9]Land, Teske, and Zheng (2009) should be commended for distinguishing between periods in Texas when the use of capital punishment appears to have been erratic and when it appears to have been systematic. But they fail to integrate this distinction into a coherently delineated behavioral model that incorporates sanctions regimes, salience, and deterrence. And, as explained above, their claims of evidence of deterrence in the systematic regime are flawed.

not provide a logical basis for linking the statistical findings back to a state's capital punishment sanction regime. Suppose, for example, that an execution event study was conducted that provided credible evidence that the execution either increased or decreased homicides that are eligible for capital punishment. Such a study would not provide the basis for altering the sanction regime to either increase or decrease the number of executions because it would not be informative about what aspect of the regime caused the execution to have the effect identified by the study.

In summary, the committee finds that adequate justifications have not been provided to demonstrate that the various time-series-based studies of capital punishment speak to the deterrence question. It is thus immaterial whether the studies purport to find evidence in favor or against deterrence. They do not rise to the level of credible evidence on the deterrent effect of capital punishment as a determinant of aggregate homicide rates and are not useful in evaluating capital punishment as a public policy.

REFERENCES

Ash, R.B., and Gardner, M.F. (1975). *Topics in Stochastic Processes.* New York: Academic Press.

Bailey, W.C. (1998). Deterrence, brutalization, and the death penalty: Another reexamination of Oklahoma's return to capital punishment. *Criminology, 36*(4), 711-733.

Becker, G.S. (1968). Crime and punishment: An economic approach. *Journal of Political Economy, 76*(2), 169-217.

Brennan, M. (2008). Capital asset pricing model. In S.N. Durlauf and L. Blume (Eds.), *The New Palgrave Dictionary of Economics* (revised ed., vol. 1, pp. 641-648). London: Palgrave MacMillan.

Charles, K.K., and Durlauf, S. (in press). Pitfalls in the use of time series methods to study deterrence and capital punishment. Submitted to *Journal of Quantitative Criminology, 28.*

Cloninger, D.O. (1992). Capital punishment and deterrence: A portfolio approach. *Applied Economics, 24*(6), 635-645.

Cloninger, D.O., and Marchesini, R. (2001). Execution and deterrence: A quasi-controlled group experiment. *Applied Economics, 33*(5), 569-576.

Cloninger, D.O., and Marchesini, R. (2006). Execution moratoriums, commutations and deterrence: The case of Illinois. *Applied Economics, 38*(9), 967-973.

Cochran, J.K., Chamlin, M.B., and Seth, M. (1994). Deterrence or brutalization—An impact assessment of Oklahoma's return to capital-punishment. *Criminology, 32*(1), 107-134.

Donohue, J.J., and Wolfers, J. (2005). Uses and abuses of empirical evidence in the death penalty debate. *Stanford Law Review, 58*(3), 791-845.

Durlauf, S., and Nagin, D. (2011). The deterrent effect of imprisonment. In P.J. Cook, J. Ludwig, and J. McCrary (Eds.), *Controlling Crime: Strategies and Tradeoffs* (pp. 43-94). Chicago: University of Chicago Press.

Federal Bureau of Investigation (2011). *Uniform Crime Reports: Estimated Murder Rate in Texas 1960-2009.* Available: http://www.ucrdatatools.gov [December 2011].

Granger, C.W.J. (1969). Investigating causal relations by econometric models and cross-spectral methods. *Econometrica, 37*(3), 424-438.

Grogger, J. (1990). The deterrent effect of capital punishment: An analysis of daily homicide counts. *Journal of the American Statistical Association, 85*(410), 295-303.

Hjalmarsson, R. (2009). Does capital punishment have a "local" deterrent effect on homicides? *American Law and Economics Review, 11*(2), 310-334.

Land, K.C., Teske, R.H.C., and Zheng, H. (2009). The short-term effects of executions on homicides: Deterrence, displacement, or both? *Criminology, 47*(4), 1,009-1,043.

Leeper, E.M., and Zha, T. (2003). Modest policy interventions. *Journal of Monetary Economics, 50*(8), 1,673-1,700.

Leeper, E.M., Sims, C.A., and Zha, T. (1996). What does monetary policy do? *Brookings Papers on Economic Activity, 1996*(2), 1-78.

Liebman, J., Fagan, J., and West, V. (2000). Capital attrition: Error rates in capital cases, 1973-1995. *Texas Law Review, 78,* 1,839-1,861.

Lucas, R. (1976). Econometric policy evaluation: A critique. *Carnegie-Rochester Conference Series on Public Policy, 1,* 19-46.

Marschak, J. (1953). Economic measurements for policy and prediction. In W.C. Hood and T.C. Koopmans (Eds.), *Studies in Econometric Method* (pp. 1-26). New Haven: Yale University Press.

Phillips, D.P. (1980). The deterrent effect of capital punishment: New evidence on an old controversy. *American Journal of Sociology, 86*(1), 138-148.

Phillips, D.P. (1982). The fluctuation of homicides after publicized executions: Reply. *American Journal of Sociology, 88*(1), 165-167.

Sims, C.A. (1972). Money, income, and causality. *American Economic Review, 62*(4), 540-552.

Sims, C.A. (1980). Macroeconomics and reality. *Econometrica, 48*(1), 1-48.

Sims, C.A., Goldfeld, S.M., and Sachs, J.D. (1982). Policy analysis with econometric models. *Brookings Papers on Economic Activity, 1982*(1), 107-164.

Stolzenberg, L., and D'Alessio, S.J. (2004). Capital punishment, execution publicity, and murder in Houston, Texas. *Journal of Criminal Law and Criminology, 94*(2), 351-379.

Texas Department of Criminal Justice. (2011). *Executed Offenders.* Available: http://www.tdcj.state.tx.us/death_row/dr_executed_offenders.html [December 2011].

Zeisel, H. (1982). The deterrent effect of capital-punishment—Comment. *American Journal of Sociology, 88*(1), 167-169.

Zimring, F.E., Fagan, J., and Johnson, D.T. (2010). Executions, deterrence, and homicide: A tale of two cities. *Journal of Empirical Legal Studies, 7*(1), 1-29.

6

Challenges to Identifying
Deterrent Effects

Researchers from diverse disciplines have contributed to the capital
punishment literature, with prominent contributions by economists,
criminologists, and sociologists. Although researchers' disciplinary
backgrounds have affected the methods used and the framing of the research questions, the failings of the capital punishment literature are not
rooted in the use of particular empirical methods or theoretical models
of criminal decision making. Rather, the failings are rooted in manifest
deficiencies related to the research data and methods and the researchers'
interpretations of results. Chapters 4 and 5 call attention, respectively, to
fundamental deficiencies in panel and time-series studies. Both approaches
share two basic deficiencies and also manifest two others to some degree.
One shared deficiency is grossly incomplete specification of the sanction regime for homicide. Even in states that make the most frequent use of capital
sanctions, noncapital sanctions are the most common sanction imposed for
a homicide conviction. No study of either type accounts for the noncapital component of the sanction regime in states with and without capital
punishment. The second basic deficiency is failure to pose a credible model
of the sanction risk perceptions of potential murderers and the behavioral
response to such perceptions. In the absence of such a model, it is difficult,
at best, to interpret data relating sanction regimes to homicide rates.

As discussed in Chapters 4 and 5, these two deficiencies are sufficient
to make existing studies uninformative about the effect of capital punishment on homicide. Both of these deficiencies are potentially correctable.
However, even if the research and data collection initiatives discussed in
this chapter are ultimately successful, research in both literatures share a

common characteristic of invoking strong, often unverifiable, assumptions in order to provide point estimates of the effect of capital punishment on homicides. A point estimate may offer the appearance of desirable certitude, but only at a high cost in credibility. Still another deficiency is inattention to potential feedbacks through which homicide rates, and crime rates more generally, may affect the specification and administration of a sanction regime while the regime simultaneously affects homicide rates. Recognition of potential feedbacks is relevant both to identify the direct effect of capital punishment on homicide rates and to predict the ultimate effect after feedbacks occur. Feedbacks affect the time-series and panel studies differently because of differences in the time frames of the data typically used in the two approaches—monthly, weekly, or even daily data in the time-series studies and annual data in the panel studies.

In light of these deficiencies, the committee has reached the following conclusion and recommendation:

> CONCLUSION AND RECOMMENDATION: The committee concludes that research to date on the effect of capital punishment on homicide is not informative about whether capital punishment decreases, increases, or has no effect on homicide rates. Therefore, the committee recommends that these studies not be used to inform deliberations requiring judgments about the effect of the death penalty on homicide. Consequently, claims that research demonstrates that capital punishment decreases or increases the homicide rate by a specified amount or has no effect on the homicide rate should not influence policy judgments about capital punishment.

The committee was disappointed to reach the conclusion that research conducted in the 30 years since the National Research Council (1978) report on this subject has not sufficiently advanced knowledge to allow a conclusion, however qualified, about the effect of the death penalty on homicide rates. Yet this is our conclusion. Some studies play the useful role, either intentionally or not, of demonstrating the fragility of their claims to have found—or not to have found—deterrent effects. However, even these studies suffer from two intrinsic shortcomings that severely limit what can be learned from them about the effect of the death penalty on homicide rates from an examination of the death penalty as it has actually been administered in the United States in the past 35 years.

Commentary on research findings often pits studies claiming to find statistically significant deterrent effects against those finding no statistically significant effects, with the latter studies sometimes interpreted as implying that there is no deterrent effect. A fundamental point of logic about hypothesis testing is that failure to reject a null hypothesis does not imply that the null hypothesis is correct. For the evidence of even a small effect to be credible, it requires a demonstration, first and foremost, that the effect is based on a sound research design. Estimates that lack credibility are not informative regardless of the consistency of their estimated size. The amount of the effect must also be small in size and estimated with good precision, for example, by being contained within a tight confidence interval.

Our mandate was not to assess whether competing hypotheses about the existence of marginal deterrence from capital punishment are plausible, but simply to assess whether the empirical studies that we have reviewed provide scientifically valid evidence. In its deliberations and in this report, the committee has made a concerted effort not to approach this question with a prior assumption about deterrence. Having reviewed the research that purports to provide useful evidence for or against the hypothesis that the death penalty affects homicide rates, we conclude that it does not provide such evidence.

We stress, however, as noted above, that a lack of evidence is not evidence for or against the hypothesis. Hence, the committee does not construe its conclusion that the existing studies are uninformative as favoring one side or the other side in the long-standing societal debate about deterrence and the death penalty.

In this chapter, we elaborate on these deficiencies that form the basis for this conclusion and cautiously offer some ideas on potential remedies. With regard to remedies, our report provides a somewhat less pessimistic perspective than did the earlier National Research Council (1978, p. 63) report: "[T]he Panel considers that research on this topic is not likely to produce findings that will or should have much influence on policymakers."

The committee does not expect that advances in collecting data on sanction regimes and obtaining knowledge of sanctions risk perceptions will come quickly or easily. However, data collection on the noncapital component of the sanction regime need not be entirely complete to be useful. And even if research on perceptions of the risk of capital punishment cannot resolve all major issues, some progress would be an important step forward. Even if these advances prove unsuccessful in providing useful information on the incremental deterrent effect of capital punishment in relation to a lengthy prison sentence, the committee believes that there are potentially major benefits from new data collection, theory, and methodology for study of the effect of noncapital sanctions on crimes not subject to the death penalty. As discussed in Chapter 1, because of the overlap in the methods and data used in studies of capital punishment and in broader studies on the effects of sanctions on crime, our charge included a provision for recommending research that might advance that broader research literature, and we do so in the rest of this chapter.

DATA ON SANCTION REGIMES

Incomplete and inaccurate data have marred research on the effect of capital punishment on homicides. The most important data problem is that studies have been based on a very incomplete specification of state sanction regimes. Part of the difficulty has been lack of conceptual agreement on how to measure the intensity of use of capital punishment. However, we see the primary problem as a complete absence of data on the noncapital sanctions that might be applied to offenders convicted of homicide. A study of capital punishment in North Carolina by Cook (2009) illustrates the importance of the problem of the absence of information on noncapital sanctions. Of 274 cases prosecuted as capital cases, only 11 resulted in a death sentence. Another 42 resulted in dismissal or a verdict of not guilty, which left 221 cases that resulted in convictions and received noncapital sanctions.

As discussed at length in Chapter 4 and below, there are sound reasons for predicting a correlation between the capital and noncapital components of a state's sanction regime. Two examples of how this might occur are the plea bargaining leverage that the threat of capital punishment may afford prosecutors and the influence of the state's political culture on the legislated design and administration of both the capital and noncapital components of the regime. Such a correlation would bias the estimated deterrent effect of capital punishment.

None of the studies we reviewed sought to measure the availability and intensity of use of the noncapital sanction alternatives for the punishment of homicide. Such alternatives may include a life sentence without the possibility of parole, a life sentence with the possibility of parole, and sentences of less than life. It would also be important to have data on the time actually served for convicted murderers who are paroled or who serve less than a life sentence.

It is currently not possible to measure noncapital sanction alternatives at the state level because the required data are not available. The data that are available include those from the Bureau of Justice Statistics (BJS), which publishes nationwide statistics on sentences for prison admissions and time served for prison releases, based on data collected as part of the National Corrections Reporting Program (NCRP) initiated in the early 1980s. More than 40 states now report annual data on sentences for admissions and time served for releases. Individual-level demographic characteristics are also reported. In principle, these data could be used to measure the actual administration of the legally authorized dimensions of most state sanction regimes, not only for murder but also for other types of crimes. The difficulty is that the data are often extremely incomplete.

In some years, states fail to report any data. Just as important, the data that are sent to BJS are often so incomplete that it is impossible to construct valid state-level measures of the administration of the sanction regime. Indeed, the committee attempted to use these data for the purposes of this report but concluded that the data gaps made their use infeasible. More complete data on the actual administration of sanction regimes might be obtained by expanding the NCRP to include all 50 states and filling the data gaps due to incomplete reporting. Alternatively, an entirely new data collection system might be desirable. Either way, the collection of more complete data on sanction regimes for murder and other crimes is feasible. The data are available: the challenge is designing and implementing an effective system for their collection.

Even if data on the actual administration of state sanction regimes were complete, they could only be used to measure how sanction regimes are actually administered. The data do not specify the *potential* sanction regime in a state—the range of sanction alternatives that are legally authorized. We are not aware of any ongoing effort to assemble data on the legislated sanction regimes of the states for murder and other crimes. Data on the legislated regime are important because they define the range of penalties that can potentially be imposed. Thus, the measurement of legally authorized sanctions by the states for homicides and other crimes may require a new data collection system.

The committee did not explore the benefits and costs of alternative approaches for measurement of state-level sanction regimes for murder. We only emphasize the vital importance of collecting these data.

> **RECOMMENDATION: The committee recommends that a concerted effort be made to collect data on the sanctions regimes faced by potential murderers, with particular attention to fixing the current absence of data on noncapital sanctions.**

As noted above, because the methods and data used to study the effect of noncapital sanctions on crimes other than murder are similar to those used in research on capital punishment, the committee's charge includes a provision that we make recommendations for advancing research on the broad effects of sanctions on crime. Thus, we also stress the vital importance of an expanded effort to collect data suitable not only for measuring sanction regimes for murder, but also for measuring sanction regimes for other major crimes.

PERCEPTIONS OF SANCTION RISKS

As emphasized in Chapter 3, it is not possible to interpret empirical evidence on the relationship of homicide rates to sanctions without understanding how potential murderers perceive sanction regimes. The committee's review of the time-series and panel studies identified fundamental deficiencies in this regard.

In the case of the time-series studies, none of them explicitly articulates a model of sanction risk perceptions. The studies are silent on whether execution events and their frequency alter perceptions of sanction regimes. Moreover, the studies do not ask whether the trend lines specified by researchers correspond to the trend line (if any) perceived by potential murderers.

Panel studies typically suppose that people who are contemplating murder perceive sanctions risks as subjective probabilities of arrest, conviction, and execution. Lacking data on these subjective probabilities, researchers presume that they are somehow based on the observable frequencies of arrest, conviction, and execution.

The fundamental problem is that perceptions of the risk of sanction are subjective, but researchers have no direct measurements of the perceptions of potential murderers. In the absence of data on risk perceptions, the research practice in the panel studies has been to use publicly available data on homicides and executions to construct statistics that purport to measure the objective risk of execution. Then, having done that, many researchers assume that potential murderers have "rational expectations." The word "rational" suggests that potential murderers carefully assess the risk of execution. What "rational expectations" actually means in practice is that researchers construct their own measures of execution risk and assume that potential murderers perceive the risk in the same way. However, the assumption of rational expectations of execution risk has no empirical foundation. Indeed, it hardly seems credible.

In Chapter 4, we discuss in detail the complications of calculating the objective risk of execution. One of these complications is that only 15 percent of individuals sentenced to death have actually been executed (since the resumption of the death penalty in 1976) and that a large fraction of death sentences are subsequently reversed. Another complication is that the volume of data on death sentences and executions available for forming perceptions depends on the size of the state. By various measures of execution risk, Delaware was at least as aggressive as Texas in its use of the death penalty. However, over the period 1976 to 2000, Delaware sentenced 28 people to death and carried out 11 executions, while Texas sentenced 753 people to death and carried out 231 executions. Still another complication is that sanction regimes are not stable due to changes in a state's political leadership, moratoriums on executions, and legal decisions. Yet another complication is that there are within-state differences in the risk of execution due to differences across counties in prosecutorial vigor in the use of the death penalty and local differences in receptivity to its application.

These many complications make clear that even with a concerted effort by careful, conscientious researchers to assemble and analyze relevant data on death sentences and executions, assessment of the evolving objective risk of execution facing a potential murderer is a daunting challenge. It is also clear that perceptions of this risk among potential murderers must at best be highly impressionistic. To make headway on whether and to what degree the death penalty affects the behavior of potential murderers, it is imperative to have knowledge about how their perceptions of execution risk are formed and then possibly revised on the basis of new information.

> RECOMMENDATION: The committee strongly recommends that a concerted effort be made to research the origins and nature of execution sanctions risk perceptions specifically and of noncapital sanctions risks more broadly.

Measurement of Perceptions

The essential task is to measure the perceptions of sanctions risks that potential murderers actually hold. How might this be done?

One possibility is to take seriously the presumption in the panel studies that people who are contemplating murder perceive sanctions risks as subjective probabilities of arrest, conviction, and execution. This possibility suggests that the risk perceptions of potential murderers be measured probabilistically.

Researchers have developed considerable experience measuring beliefs probabilistically in broad population surveys. Manski (2004) reviews the history in several disciplines, describes the emergence of the modern literature, summarizes applications, and discusses open issues. Among the major U.S. platforms for collection of such data, the Health and Retirement Study (HRS) has periodically elicited probabilistic expectations of retirement, bequests, and mortality from multiple cohorts of older Americans (see, e.g., Hurd and McGarry, 1995, 2002; Hurd, Smith, and Zissimopoulos, 2004). The Survey of Economic Expectations (SEE) has asked repeated population cross sections to state the percent chance that they will lose their jobs, have health insurance, or be victims of crime in the year ahead (see, e.g., Dominitz and Manski, 1997; Manski and Straub, 2000). The National Longitudinal Survey of Youth 1997 has periodically asked young people about the chance that they will become a parent, be arrested, or complete schooling (see, e.g., Fischhoff et al., 2000; Lochner, 2007). Examples of victimization and arrest questions include, "What do you think is the percent chance that your home will be burglarized in the next year?" "What do you think is the percent chance that you will be arrested in the next year?" Researchers have learned from these and other surveys that most people have little difficulty, once the concept is introduced, in using subjective probabilities to express the likelihood they place on future events relevant to their lives.

However, success in measuring beliefs probabilistically within the general public does not imply that survey research could similarly measure the sanction risk perceptions of potential murderers. A major issue when initiating study of this type is to obtain data from the relevant population, in this case, the population of potential murderers. Theoretically, most people who would be legally eligible to be executed (e.g., are not juveniles or of very low intelligence) are also physically capable of committing a murder and thereby are potential murderers. The reality, however, is that the probability of most people committing a murder is so small that as a practical matter it can be treated as zero. Even the probabilities of people committing other serious crimes, such as robbery and burglary, while likely greater, are still extremely small. Thus, when using the term "potential murderer," one means that part of population with a non-negligible risk of committing murder.

Thus, the first step and an important prerequisite for a program of research on sanction risk perceptions is to define the relevant population of potential murderers and, more generally, potential criminals. Such a definition will be required to devise cost-effective sampling strategies for interviewing people with nontrivial risks of committing crimes. We expect that one important segment of the relevant population is people with criminal records. The correlation between past and future offending is among the best documented empirical regularities in criminology (National Research Council, 1986; West and Farrington, 1973; Wolfgang, 1958). In the case of murder, for example, Cook, Ludwig, and Braga (2005) found that 43 percent of murderers in Illinois had a felony conviction.

Some may question the feasibility of collecting data on the sanction risk perceptions and criminal behavior of individuals with prior histories of serious crimes, especially if subjects are repeatedly interviewed for the purpose of obtaining longitudinal data. Longitudinal data are useful to study how offending experience and external events, such as police crackdowns or policy changes, affect sanction risk perceptions. However, experience demonstrates that, with sufficient diligence, it is feasible to collect longitudinal data on highly crime-prone people.

A leading example is the Pathways to Desistance Project (Mulvey, 2011), a two-site longitudinal study of desistance from crime among serious adolescent offenders. The project recruited 1,354 adolescents from the Philadelphia and Phoenix juvenile and adult court systems who had been adjudicated as delinquent or found guilty of a serious felony and were 14 to 17 years old at the time that they committed the offense. For the first 4 years of the study, interviews were conducted at 6-month intervals and for the next 3 years the interviews were annual. The retention rate was quite high, with 87 percent of the subjects interviewed in at least 8 of the 10 interview cycles. Respondents were asked about their perceptions of sanctions risks, among other things. The success of this project indicates that collection of data on sanction risk perceptions from crime-prone populations is feasible with a sustained commitment among a cadre of researchers and with the availability of funding.

Apel (in press) reviews the existing research that measures perceptions of sanction risks. Although there have been a scattering of suggestive studies, there has not yet been systematic large-scale research on the subject. Moreover, there has been no research at all on the specific question of perceptions of the sanction risk associated with commission of murder.

With so much to learn, we think it prudent for research to proceed sequentially. A good beginning would be small-scale studies that include one-on-one cognitive interviews with respondents in the relevant population of potential murderers. These interviews, taking the form of structured conversations, would explore the feasibility and usefulness of probabilistic and other modes of questioning about sanction risk perception. The lessons learned from this exploratory research would inform the design of larger studies, the aim being to eventually develop a program of survey research that would regularly measure the perceptions of the sanction risk held by potential murderers and by potential criminals more generally.

The committee is not confident that measurement of the sanctions risk perceptions of potential murderers can succeed in producing information useful to the study of deterrence, but one cannot be sure unless the effort is made. As demonstrated by the discussion in Chapters 4 and 5, the alternative of continuing to make unfounded assumptions about these perceptions is not useful. Measurement of sanction risk perceptions may enable deterrence research to make progress that thus far has not been possible in the absence of data.

The committee is more optimistic about the feasibility and usefulness of measuring perceptions of sanctions risks among potential criminals more broadly. This greater optimism has two bases. First, homicide is the least frequent of the crimes included in the "Part 1-Crime Index" of the Federal Bureau of Investigation (FBI), which also includes rape, robbery, aggravated assault, burglary, larceny, and auto theft. More people commit all the other crimes than commit homicides. Thus, it will probably be easier to survey sizable numbers of potential perpetrators of these crimes than of potential murderers. The National Survey of Youth, for example, already surveys youth and young adults about their involvement in such crimes as theft, selling drugs, and assault.

Second, perpetrators who are apprehended for crimes less serious than murder are far less likely to receive lengthy prison sentences, particularly if they are juveniles. Thus, these people have more opportunity to learn about sanction risk on the basis of personal experience, a source of information that may be vital to formation of sanction risk perceptions.

Inference on Perceptions from Homicide Rates Following Executions

As a complement to research that directly measures perceptions, some committee members believe that study of homicide rates immediately following execution events might also provide useful evidence of the perceptions of potential murderers. As discussed in Chapter 5, the time-series research has largely been devoted to the question of whether homicide rates change in the immediate aftermath of an execution. For the reasons detailed in that chapter, the committee concluded that existing studies were not informative about whether capital punishment affects homicide rates, in part because of the absence of any measure of perceptions.

The committee considered at length whether future research on execution events, if properly conducted, might be informative about whether homicide rates, at least in the short term, are responsive to execution events. We concluded that at best the information to be gleaned from this type of research would be limited and fall far short of establishing whether capital punishment increases, decreases, or has no effect on homicide rates. Even if a short-term impact could be established, it would be difficult to determine whether homicides were actually prevented or simply displaced in time. More fundamentally, execution event studies cannot speak to the question of whether and how the state's overall sanction regime affects the homicide rate. For example, a null finding from an event study would leave open the possibility that a death penalty regime had a deterrent effect relative to a regime that precluded the death penalty or more narrowly prescribed its applicability. It is important to note that any *one* execution would only have a deterrent effect if it changed potential murderers' perceptions of the likelihood of an execution, which is not necessarily the case.

Acknowledging these limitations, some committee members nonetheless argue that if a well-done event study did produce evidence of an effect—whether positive or negative and no matter how temporary—that result would be of considerable interest. It would demonstrate that potential murderers as a group are actually paying attention to the state's actions and are influenced by them. In short, it would confirm a threshold condition for there to be a deterrent or brutalization effect and invite further inquiry. Other committee members are not convinced of the value of establishing this threshold condition or are not convinced that any study of this sort could make a convincing case that it had isolated a causal effect of executions.

IDENTIFYING EFFECTS:
FEEDBACKS AND UNOBSERVED CONFOUNDERS

Even with better data and information on sanction regimes and perceptions of sanction risks, formidable difficulties remain to understanding the impact of the death penalty on homicide. With only observational (nonexperimental) data on capital punishment and homicides, researchers must face the fundamental problem that the data alone cannot reveal the counterfactual question of interest: What would have happened if the death penalty not been applied in a "treatment" state or if the death penalty had been applied in a "control" state? Although this counterfactual-outcomes problem is common to all observational studies of cause and effect, it has long been understood to be particularly problematic for understanding the deterrent effect of the death penalty. A capital punishment regime evolves over time as a result, among other things, of a complex interplay of crime trends, social norms, criminal justice budgets, and election results. This context makes it very difficult to identify the effects of the capital sanction regime alone.

To better understand these issues, we highlight three related identification problems that complicate efforts to draw credible inferences on the effect of capital punishment on homicides. The first, referred to as a feedback effect, arises when homicide rates may directly affect the capital sanction regime. The second, referred to as the omitted variable problem, arises when variables that are jointly associated with the sanction regime and homicide rate are either unknown or unobserved. The third, referred to as an equilibrium effect, arises when the capital sanction regime may directly affect other aspects of the criminal justice system, including, most notably, noncapital sanction policies.

Feedback Effects

Deterrence research conducted in the early 1970s (Carr-Hill and Stern, 1973; Ehrlich, 1975; Sjoquist, 1973) recognized the possibility of *feedbacks* or *simultaneity* whereby crime rates may affect the sanction risk and severity even as the sanction risk and severity may affect crime rates. The nature of such feedbacks is not well understood, but there are good reasons for believing that feedbacks are present and may be substantial.

To illustrate the problem, suppose that in a particular state during a particular year there is an exogenous increase in the rate of homicide. If, given the additional workload and resulting strain on resources, district attorneys were more reluctant to pursue the death penalty, a continuing upward trend in homicides would appear to show that a reduction in the probability of a death sentence is associated with an increase in homicides—a result compatible with a deterrent effect. But suppose instead that the upward trend in homicides resulted in greater public concern about violence and hence a greater willingness on the part of juries in capital cases to choose a death sentence rather than a life sentence. A continuing upward trend in homicides would then appear to show that an increase in capital sanctions is associated with an increase in homicide, a result compatible with a "brutalization" effect. In both these scenarios, the important fact is that the homicide trends influenced the sanction regime. These particular feedbacks are hypothetical, and indeed the very presence of feedbacks has yet to be documented. Still, there are plausible reasons for believing that feedbacks are present and possibly substantial in magnitude. If so, they increase the difficulty of identifying deterrent effects.

Omitted Variables

The second and related problem arises when unobserved changes in the social, political, and economic environment may have an impact on *both* capital sanctions and other aspects of the sanction regime. For example, a political shift that results in the election of "law and order" legislators may increase criminal justice resources and produce a broad shift toward greater severity in sentencing, with some effects on the homicide rate. In this case, changes in the capital sanction regime may be spuriously related to the changes in the homicide rate through the associated changes in the noncapital sanction regime. If variables that are jointly associated with the sanction regime and homicide rates are omitted from statistical models of the effect of capital punishment on homicide, then estimates of the deterrent effect will be biased.

The panel research includes studies that recognize and attempt to address the inferential consequences of feedback effects and omitted variable problems. As discussed in Chapter 4, these attempts have not been successful in advancing plausible identification strategies to these problems. In particular, the instrumental variables used in these analyses do not plausibly meet criteria for a valid instrument. The two key criteria are that (1) on average, sanction levels vary as a function of the instrumental variable but (2) on average, the crime rate at a given sanction level does not vary as a function of the instrumental variable. In Chapter 4, we argue that the instrumental variable used in the studies do not meet the second test. This criticism echoes the conclusions of the earlier National Research Council report (1978). Thus, the same elementary error in identification is being made in contemporary research on the deterrent effect of capital punishment that was made decades ago by early deterrence researchers.

The Equilibrium Effect

We now turn to a third causal process that makes identification problematic, one that has been largely ignored in the research yet is of unique salience to studying the deterrent effect of capital punishment. For capital punishment, changes in the probability of capital sanctions may cause changes to other aspects of the sanctions regime. To illustrate the problem, consider two examples. First, a district attorney who can credibly threaten an accused homicide defendant with the death penalty may have greater bargaining leverage than one who lacks this threat; as a result, the defendants in the former situation may be more willing to plead guilty to first-degree murder with an agreement that their sentence will be life imprisonment rather than death (Cook, 2009; Kuziemko, 2006). Thus, a district attorney who is willing to devote resources to capital prosecutions may end up achieving more severe noncapital sentences, and the two types of sentences are intrinsically linked.

There may also be a negative linkage, if, for example, a district attorney's proclivity to seek the death penalty in homicide cases comes at the cost of reduced prosecutorial resources available for other cases.[1] Due to resource constraints and the additional costs of prosecuting capital murder cases rather than noncapital murder cases, emphasis on capital cases may diminish prosecutorial effectiveness in noncapital cases. The result in that situation may be that the more intense capital regime is achieved at the cost of reduced sentencing (and more dismissals) for the majority of homicide cases that are not capital. These potential links between capital and noncapital sentences make it difficult to isolate the deterrent effect of the threat of execution for homicide.

The equilibrium process, whereby capital and noncapital sanction policies are jointly related and jointly influence the outcome of interest, poses a qualitatively different challenge to identification than the first two. In principle, if the probability that a homicide case would result in a death sentence was randomly assigned across jurisdictions, then the identification problems resulting from feedbacks or omitted variables (discussed above) would be solved. What would remain, however, is the potential difficulty in isolating the deterrent effect of the death penalty by itself from the changes in the overall sanction regime that are influenced by the availability and use of the death penalty.

---

[1]Numerous studies have documented that the prosecution of capital homicide cases is far more costly than noncapital homicide cases: see, for example, Roman, Chalfin, and Knight (2009) in Maryland; Cook (2009) in North Carolina; and Alarcón and Mitchell (2011) and the California Commission on the Fair Administration of Justice (2008) in California. Due to resource constraints, emphasis on capital cases may diminish prosecutorial effectiveness in noncapital cases.

Knowledge of the entire system, however, is not a necessary require-ment for learning about the overall impact of the capital sanction regime. For some questions, the effects of the death penalty on sentence bargain-ing and on administrative resource constraints are an intrinsic part of the mechanism by which a capital regime affects murder rates. Consider, for example, a case in which a judicial ruling terminates the use of the death penalty for some category of homicides. It would be of considerable interest to have a reliable estimate of the overall effect of this reform on the murder rate, even if it is not possible to distinguish among the various mechanisms (reduction in the probability of a death sentence, weaker bargaining posi-tion by the district attorney, or increased court resources available for the average case) that led to that effect. Still, this sort of "black box" estimate is not satisfactory if the goal is to estimate the effect of the threat of execu-tion, in part because the ancillary effects of the administration of the death penalty can be generated by other means, such as changes in court budgets.

Is a more reliable approach to identifying the deterrent effect of capital punishment possible? Part of the solution may be to develop a better un-derstanding of the factors that affect sanction regimes, including possible feedbacks from homicide or other crime patterns. The earlier National Research Council report (1978, p. 47) observed: "Knowledge of the effect of crime on the behavior of the criminal justice system is still extremely limited." This conclusion is still true today, 30 years later. The 1978 report went on to observe: "While the seeming dearth of untainted identification restrictions may reflect the fact that none exist, it is certainly as likely that it simply reflects our ignorance of the determinants of sanctions" (p. 48). Three decades later this committee observes that both of these assessments apply to contemporary research on deterrence.

As noted above, the 1978 report urged more research on the sanction-generation process for the purpose of accumulating a knowledge base that might reveal approaches to plausible identification. Although knowledge of the sanction-generation process is not required for identification of overall effects of certain relevant regime changes, that knowledge may be useful in determining the validity of a proposed identification method. Also, as a practical matter, some committee members believe that without better knowledge of sanction generation, the prospects for credible identifica-tion are small. Committee members holding this perspective argue that a deeper institutional and theoretical knowledge of sanction process would materially increase the chances of researchers' becoming aware of credible sources of identification and that without such knowledge the chances for credible identification are remote. Other committee members are less pes-simistic that a chance event or insight might provide a basis for credible identification.

However credible identification might ultimately be achieved, the committee fully endorses another observation from the earlier report (National Research Council, 1978, p. 49):

> It must be noted, however, that identification restrictions cannot be manufactured. If the process generating the data is truly one that leaves the crime function unidentified, then persistent attempts to produce identifying restrictions because of the desire to estimate the deterrent effect will only produce different kinds of error. Even if all such attempts found a "deterrent" effect, no conclusion would be warranted unless some of them used validly based identification restrictions.

ADDRESSING MODEL UNCERTAINTY WITH WEAKER ASSUMPTIONS

The persistent problems that researchers have had in providing meaningful answers about the deterrent effect of capital punishment is unsurprising once one recognizes that this body of empirical research rests on strong and unverified assumptions. Although, in practice, researchers often recognize and acknowledge that their assumptions may not hold, they are defended as necessary to provide meaningful answers and in order to make inferences. But the use of strong assumptions hides the problem that very little is understood about the process that may link capital punishment to future crimes.

The different findings in the deterrence research reflect different choices of assumptions, most of which cannot be supported by strong a priori justifications. As documented throughout this report, many of the assumptions used in the research on the deterrent effect of capital punishment are not credible. Furthermore, the state of social science knowledge does not support a unique model that can be used to identify the effects of capital punishment under the current U.S. sanction regime or to permit the evaluation of deterrence under alternative regimes. The study of deterrence is plagued by model uncertainty.

The failure of the existing research to address the issue of model uncertainly is evident in the debate initiated by Donohue and Wolfers (2005), who challenged claims of deterrence by a broad set of researchers. Much of their challenge involved demonstrations of how small changes in the models used in the various studies led to very different estimates of deterrence effects, in some case changing from positive to negative or vice versa, and in others eliminating statistical significance. Some of their exercises altered the set of observations over which the analysis had been conducted; in other cases they changed the choice of control or instrumental variables.

Although Donohue and Wolfers provide useful evidence of the sensitivity of many claims of deterrence to model assumptions, their demonstration begs the question of how to adjudicate their findings relative to the papers they critique. This may be seen in two of the rejoinders that have been written to their study. Dezhbakhsh and Rubin (2011) and Mocan and Gittings (2010) provide a large number of modifications of their baseline homicide regressions and argue that deterrence effects generally appear in them. However, they fail to provide any guidance as to what is learned from the specifications that are inconsistent with their claim of evidence of deterrence. Rather, the authors' claims are based on ad hoc choices of alternative model specifications; there is no systematic construction of the models from which to draw inferences. That changes in a given statistical model change the output of the model is hardly unique to the studies of capital punishment and deterrence literature. The problem is that there have been almost no serious attempts to reconcile the many different findings reported in the research.

Given this existing uncertainty, how might research proceed? Certainly, research aimed at reducing model uncertainty would be useful. To that end, the committee proposed, above, developing data and research on sanction regimes and perceptions of sanction risk. Another complementary and potentially useful approach would be to explicitly account for model uncertainty when drawing inferences on the impact of capital punishment. Rather than continue with the conventional practice of assuming whatever it takes to achieve point identification, and then providing ad hoc justifications for particular sets of assumptions to justify a given model, deterrent studies might instead consider what can be learned when explicitly recognizing model uncertainty. Although the resulting inferences may reflect a certain degree of ambiguity about the effects of capital punishment on homicides, those inferences will necessarily possess greater credibility.

To explore the idea of addressing model uncertainty, the committee commissioned papers illustrating application of two complementary research paradigms—the model averaging approach and the partial identification approach.

Model Averaging

Model averaging, though based on earlier work (Bates and Granger, 1969; Leamer, 1978), developed theoretically, algorithmically, and as an applied technique in the mid-1990s (examples include Chatfield, 1995; Draper, 1995; Draper et al., 1993; Raftery, Madigan, and Hoeting, 1997). The model averaging approach constructs a probability distribution for a range of estimates of the deterrent effect of capital punishment, and the researcher constructs this distribution to reflect the researcher's own or others experts' prior beliefs about the probability that a given model is valid. By asking what can be learned by combining the information obtained across a wide range of models, model averaging methods provide a natural way to make empirical claims robust to the details of uncertain model specifications.

This technique has recently been used in two studies of capital punishment: Cohen-Cole et al. (2009) and Durlauf, Fu, and Navarro (in press). These studies apply the modeling average approach to various specifications that have appeared in the research on capital punishment and deterrence. Cohen-Cole et al. (2009) use this method to adjudicate the different findings of Dezhbakhsh, Rubin, Shepherd (2003) and Donohue and Wolfers (2005). Durlauf, Fu, and Navarro (in press), whose paper was written for this committee, consider a range of models based on alternative substantive assumptions that have appeared in the research, including, for example, how to measure subjective arrest, sentencing, and execution probabilities and whether the deterrent effect of capital punishment differs across states. These two papers aim to understand how different assumptions matter and whether differences in assumptions render deterrence estimates fragile. In both papers, the researchers find that model uncertainty swamps the informational content about deterrent effects. That is, after accounting for the modeling uncertainty, the empirical evidence does not reveal whether capital punishment increases or decreases homicides.

As an example of this result, consider the Cohen-Cole et al. (2009) analysis of the models in Dezhbakhsh, Rubin, and Shepherd (2003) and Donohue and Wolfers (2005). Dezhbakhsh, Rubin, and Shepherd (2003) report, under their preferred specification, a statistically significant point estimate of 18 lives saved for each execution. However, when all of the different specifications spanned in the two papers are given probability weights, Cohen-Cole et al. estimate an approximate 95 percent confidence interval on the number of lives saved per execution of [–24, 124]: see Figure 6-1, which is from Cohen-Cole et al. The figure illustrates the model uncertainty by providing a weighted histogram of the estimated net lives saved for all of the models considered. For the case illustrated in this histogram, the posterior probability for the models with point estimates suggest that deterrence is 72 percent, but there is substantial bunching around 0, the individual estimates vary widely, and there is a nontrivial probability on models that suggest a large increase in homicides associated with executions (a probability 0.15 of point estimates of 20 or more homicides). Thus, the heterogeneity of the model-specific estimates makes it impossible to draw strong qualitative conclusions about the deterrent effect of capital punishment.

The model averaging approach provides a formal and elegant Bayesian method for incorporating uncertainty about the correct modeling assumptions into inferential methods. This approach can be effectively used to illustrate the importance of different assumptions and the fragility of the estimates to these assumptions, as is done in Cohen-Cole et al. (2009) and

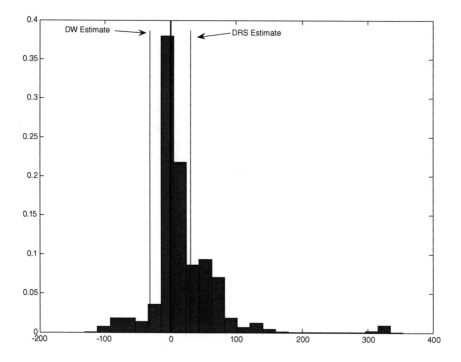

FIGURE 6-1 Weighted histogram of the net lives saved by the death penalty.
NOTES: The figure includes models for each of the DRS (Dezhbakhsh, Rubin, and Shepherd, 2003) categories. The weights are the posterior model probabilities (Bayes factors). The DRS and DW (Donohue and Wolfers, 2005) lines correspond to the individual model from each with the largest and smallest number of lives saved, respectively. The unweighted histogram is similar.
SOURCE: Cohen-Cole et al. (2009, Figure 1). Used with permission.

Durlauf, Fu, and Navarro (in press). The approach depends on research-ers' specifications of the model space and prior over that model space, over which there may be disagreement. Such disagreement should not obscure an essential strength of the model averaging approach: model averaging pro-vides an approach for systematically exploring sensitivity over an explicitly defined model space.

Ultimately, this approach might also be used to infer the effect of the death penalty on homicides. However, for this purpose, a key challenge would be selecting a set of models to include in the averaging and provid-ing a prior probability distribution over this set that is plausible. The ap-proach presumes that the range of models included in the averaging routine includes the correct model that accurately describes the real world and, moreover, that the researcher can provide informed prior beliefs about the probability that each model is valid. In the context of the research on capital punishment, we have found no reason to believe that the existing range of point-identified models includes the correct one, and there is currently little basis for assigning probabilities to the correctness of each model in the literature. As discussed in Chapter 4, the committee did not find the instrumental variables used in the existing research to be credible. If the existing models are all invalid, using the modeling averaging approach to produce interpretable deterrence estimates can be problematic.[2] With uncertainty about the model space and the prior probabilities, either research efforts to construct informative priors or research showing the sensitivity of the posterior to different prior distributions may be useful.

Partial Identification

Partial identification methods provide an alternative approach for reducing the dependence of claims of a deterrence effect on arbitrary assumptions. Rather than start with a particular set of point-identified models and prior beliefs about the probability that each model is valid, both as defined by the researcher, one might instead begin by directly considering what can be inferred under a set of weak assumptions that may possess greater credibility. A natural starting point, for example, is to examine what can be learned in the absence of any assumptions. What do the data alone reveal? Under these weaker assumptions, deterrent effects may not be point identified, but they will be partially identified, with bounds rather than point estimates. Thus, the partial identification approach formalizes the inherent tradeoff between the strength of the maintained assumptions and the credibility of inferences (see Manski, 2003).

The partial identification methodology has been developed and applied over the past 20 years, beginning with Manski (1989, 1990). In an early application to criminal justice policy, Manski and Nagin (1998) studied sentencing and recidivism of juvenile offenders in the state of Utah and demonstrated how partial identification can be used to produce more credible inferences than had previously been produced. Youth in Utah faced a policy that gave judges the discretion to order varying sentences. Using this discretion, judges sentenced some offenders to residential confinement and sentenced other offenders to no confinement. A policy question of potential

---

[2]The Cohen-Cole et al. exercise (2009) was narrow in that it considered the smallest model space one could generate around the different assumptions in Donohue and Wolfers (2005) and Dezhbakhsh, Rubin, and Shepherd (2003). One can easily argue that for a full model averaging analysis, other models warrant a priori consideration. However, one could also argue that some of the models considered in Cohen-Cole et al. should not have been included, given a prior probability of 0.

interest was to compare recidivism under that policy with the recidivism that would occur under a policy proposal that removed judicial discretion and instead mandated that all offenders be sentenced to confinement. The study showed how bounds of varying width on the existing treatment effect which allows judges' discretion could be achieved by combining data on outcomes under the status quo with relatively weak assumptions regarding the manner in which (1) judges have made sentencing decisions and (2) criminality was affected by sentencing.

More recently, in a paper written for this committee, Manski and Pepper (in press) illustrate the partial identification approach in a relatively simple setting by examining the effect of death penalty statutes on the national homicide rate (per 100,000) over 2 years, 1975-1977: 1975 was the last full year of the federal moratorium on death penalty, and 1977 was the first full year after the moratorium was lifted. In 1975, the death penalty was illegal throughout the country; and in 1977, 32 states had legal death penalty statutes. Over this 2-year period, homicide rates in the 32 states that had adopted a death penalty statute in 1977 decreased by 0.6; in the remaining states, the homicide rates decreased by 1.1. It has been common in the relevant research to report the difference-in-difference estimate, which in this case is 0.5 (−0.6 + 1.1), as a point estimate of the effect of capital punishment on the national homicide rate. This interpretation suggests that the death penalty increases crime, but Manski and Pepper (in press) show that this difference-in-difference form only point identifies the impact of the death penalty under a number of strong assumptions, most notably that the effect is assumed to be homogeneous across states and dates. Under weaker assumptions that allow the deterrent effect to vary across states, the average effect of the death penalty is only partially identified, and it was found to lie in the interval [−1.9, 8.3]. Under still weaker assumptions under which the effect of the death penalty is allowed to vary over time, the bounds widen further. Thus, under these weaker models, the average treatment effect of capital punishment is bounded, but the data do not identify whether the death penalty increases or decreases homicides.

The committee does not endorse the specific findings of the recent studies applying the model averaging or partial identification approaches. These studies are largely illustrative and do not address many of the key problems identified throughout this report. Most notably, they do not define the counterfactual sanction regime and do not address the issue of how potential murderers perceive sanction risks. Still, these studies serve as a starting point for future research that might inform the debate on the death penalty. Rather than imposing the strong but unsupported assumptions required to identify the effect of capital punishment on homicides in a single model or an ad hoc set of similar models, approaches that explicitly account for model uncertainty may provide a constructive way for research to provide credible albeit incomplete answers. The basic insight is that with model uncertainty, the identification of deterrent effects need not be an all-or-nothing undertaking: the available data and credible assumptions may yield partial conclusions.

Some people may find partial conclusions unappealing and be tempted to impose strong assumptions in order to obtain definitive answers. We caution against this reaction. Imposing strong but untenable assumptions cannot truly resolve inferential problems. Rather, it simply replaces the modeling uncertainty with uncertainty associated with the underlying assumptions. We have seen this repeatedly in the literature on the death penalty. The earlier Panel on Research on Deterrent and Incapacitative Effects recognized this when it concluded (National Research Council, 1978, p. 63) "research on this topic is not likely to produce findings that will or should have much influence on policymakers." Today, more than 30 years later, perhaps the primary lesson learned from the latest round of empirical research on the deterrent effect of the death penalty is that researchers and policy makers must cope with ambiguity. Explicitly recognizing and accounting for this uncertainty seems like the only hope of moving forward.

RECOMMENDATION: The committee recommends further investigation of the effects of capital punishment using assumptions that are weaker and more credible than those that have traditionally been invoked by empirical researchers.

REFERENCES

Alarcón, A.L., and Mitchell, P.M. (2011). Executing the will of the voters?: A roadmap to mend or end the California legislature's multi-billion-dollar death penalty debacle. *Loyola of Los Angeles Law Review, 44*(Special), S41-S224.

Apel, R. (in press). Sanctions, perceptions, and crime: Implications for criminal deterrence. Submitted to *Journal of Quantitative Criminology, 28.*

Bates, J.M., and Granger, C.W.J. (1969). The combination of forecasts. *Operational Research Quarterly, 20*(4), 451-468.

California Commission on the Fair Administration of Justice. (2008). *Report and Recommendations on the Administration of the Death Penalty in California.* Sacramento: Author.

Carr-Hill, R.A., and Stern, N.H. (1979). *Crime, the Police and Criminal Statistics: An Analysis of Official Statistics for England and Wales Using Econometric Methods.* New York: Academic Press.

Chatfield, C. (1995). Model uncertainty, data mining and statistical inference. *Journal of the Royal Statistical Society Series A-Statistics in Society, 158*(3), 419-466.

Cohen-Cole, E., Durlauf, S., Fagan, J., and Nagin, D. (2009). Model uncertainty and the deterrent effect of capital punishment. *American Law and Economics Review, 11*(2), 335-369.

Cook, P.J. (2009). Potential savings from abolition of the death penalty in North Carolina. *American Law and Economics Review, 11*(2), 498-529.

Cook, P.J., Ludwig, J., and Braga, A.A. (2005). Criminal records of homicide offenders. *The Journal of the American Medical Association, 294*(5), 598-601.

Dezhbakhsh, H., and Rubin, P.H. (2011). From the "econometrics of capital punishment" to the "capital punishment" of econometrics: On the use and abuse of sensitivity analysis. *Applied Economics, 43*(25), 3,655-3,670.

Dezhbakhsh, H., Rubin, P.H., and Shepherd, J.M. (2003). Does capital punishment have a deterrent effect? New evidence from postmoratorium panel data. *American Law and Economics Review, 5,* 344-376.

Dominitz, J., and Manski, C.F. (1997). Perceptions of economic insecurity - evidence from the survey of economic expectations. *Public Opinion Quarterly, 61*(2), 261-287.

Donohue, J.J., and Wolfers, J. (2005). Uses and abuses of empirical evidence in the death penalty debate. *Stanford Law Review, 58*(3), 791-845.

Draper, D. (1995). Assessment and propagation of model uncertainty. *Journal of the Royal Statistical Society Series B-Methodological, 57*(1), 45-97.

Draper, D., Hodges, J.S., Mallows, C.L., and Pregibon, D. (1993). Exchangeability and data-analysis. *Journal of the Royal Statistical Society Series A-Statistics in Society, 156*(1), 9-37.

Durlauf, S., Fu, C., and Navarro, S. (in press). Capital punishment and deterrence: Understanding disparate results. Submitted to *Journal of Quantitative Criminology, 28.*

Ehrlich, I. (1975). Deterrent effect of capital punishment—Question of life and death. *American Economic Review, 65*(3), 397-417.

Fischhoff, B., Parker, A.M., De Bruin, W.B., Downs, J., Palmgren, C., Dawes, R., and Manski, C.F. (2000). Teen expectations for significant life events. *Public Opinion Quarterly, 64*(2), 189-205.

Hurd, M., and McGarry, K. (1995). Evaluation of the subjective probabilities of survival in the Health and Retirement Study. *Journal of Human Resources, 30*(5), S268-S292.

Hurd, M.D., and McGarry, K. (2002). The predictive validity of subjective probabilities of survival. *The Economic Journal, 112*(482), 966-985.

Hurd, M.D., Smith, J.P., and Zissimopoulos, J.M. (2004). The effects of subjective survival on retirement and social security claiming. *Journal of Applied Econometrics, 19*(6), 761-775.

Kuziemko, I. (2006). Does the threat of the death penalty affect plea bargaining in murder cases? Evidence from New York's 1995 reinstatement of capital punishment. *American Law and Economics Review, 8*(1), 116-142.

Leamer, E.E. (1978). *Specification Searches: Ad Hoc Inference with Nonexperimental Data.* New York: Wiley.

Lochner, L. (2007). Individual perceptions of the criminal justice system. *American Economic Review, 97*(1), 444-460.

Manski, C.F. (1989). Anatomy of the selection problem. *Journal of Human Resources, 24*(3), 343-360.

Manski, C.F. (1990). Nonparametric bounds on treatment effects. *American Economic Review, 80*(2), 319-323.

Manski, C.F. (2003). *Partial Identification of Probability Distributions.* New York: Springer.

Manski, C.F. (2004). Measuring expectations. *Econometrica, 72*(5), 1,329-1,376.

Manski, C.F., and Nagin, D.S. (1998). Bounding disagreements about treatment effects: A case study of sentencing and recidivism. *Sociological Methodology, 28*(1), 99-137.

Manski, C.F., and Pepper, J. (in press). Deterrence and the death penalty: Partial identification analysis using repeated cross sections. Submitted to *Journal of Quantitative Criminology, 28.*

Manski, C.F., and Straub, J.D. (2000). Worker perceptions of job insecurity in the mid-1990s—Evidence from the survey of economic expectations. *Journal of Human Resources, 35*(3), 447-479.

Mocan, N., and Gittings, K. (2010). The impact of incentives on human behavior: Can we make it disappear? The case of the death penalty. In R.E.S. Di Tella and E. Schargrodsky (Eds.), *The Economics of Crime: Lessons for and from Latin America* (pp. 379-420). Chicago: University of Chicago Press.

Mulvey, E.P. (2011). *Highlights from Pathways to Desistance: A Longitudinal Study of Serious Adolescent Offenders. Juvenile Justice Fact Sheet.* Washington, DC: U.S. Department of Justice.

National Research Council. (1978). *Deterrence and Incapacitation: Estimating the Effects of Criminal Sanctions on Crime Rates.* Panel on Research on Deterrent and Incapacitative Effects. A. Blumstein, J. Cohen, and D. Nagin (Eds.), Committee on Research on Law Enforcement and Criminal Justice. Assembly of Behavioral and Social Sciences. Washington, DC: National Academy Press.

National Research Council. (1986). *Criminal Careers and "Career Criminals."* Panel on Research on Criminal Careers, A. Blumstein, J. Cohen, J.A. Roth, and C.A. Visher (Eds.), Committee on Research on Law Enforcement and the Administration of Justice. Commission on Behavioral and Social Sciences and Education. Washington, DC: National Academy Press.

Raftery, A.E., Madigan, D., and Hoeting, J.A. (1997). Bayesian model averaging for linear regression models. *Journal of the American Statistical Association, 92*(437), 179-191.

Roman, J.K., Chalfin, A.J., and Knight, C.R. (2009). Reassessing the cost of the death penalty using quasi-experimental methods: Evidence from Maryland. *American Law and Economics Review, 11*(2), 530-574.

Sjoquist, D.L. (1973). Property crime and economic behavior: Some empirical results. *American Economic Review, 63*(3), 439-446.

West, D.J., and Farrington, D.P. (1973). *Who Becomes Delinquent? Second Report of the Cambridge Study in Delinquent Development.* London: Heinemann Educational.

Wolfgang, M.E. (1958). *Patterns in Criminal Homicide.* Philadelphia: University of Pennsylvania Press.

Appendix

Biographical Sketches of
Committee Members and Staff

Daniel S. Nagin (*Chair*) is Teresa and H. John Heinz III university professor of public policy and statistics in the Heinz College at Carnegie Mellon University. His research focuses on the evolution of criminal and antisocial behaviors over the life course, the deterrent effect of criminal and noncriminal penalties on illegal behaviors, and the development of statistical methods for analyzing longitudinal data. His work has appeared in such diverse outlets as the *American Economic Review,* the *American Sociological Review,* the *Journal of the American Statistical Association, Archives of General Psychiatry, Psychological Methodology, Law & Society Review,* and *Stanford Law Review*. He is an elected fellow of the American Society of Criminology and of the American Association for the Advancement of Science, and he was the 2006 recipient of the American Society of Criminology's Edwin H. Sutherland Award. He holds a Ph.D. from the H. John Heinz III School of Public Policy and Management at Carnegie Mellon University.

Kerwin K. Charles is the Edwin and Betty L. Bergman distinguished service professor in the Harris School of public policy studies at the University of Chicago and a research associate at the National Bureau of Economic Research. His research focuses on a range of subjects in the broad area of applied microeconomics, including how mandated minimum marriage ages affects young people's marriage and migration behavior; the effect of racial composition of neighborhoods on the social connections people make; differences in visible consumption across racial and ethnic groups; the effect of retirement on subjective well-being; and the propagation of wealth across generations within a family. His recent work has studied the degree

125

to which prejudice can account for wages and employment differences by race and gender. He has a Ph.D. from Cornell University.

Philip J. Cook is the ITT/Sanford professor of public policy and professor of economics and sociology at Duke University. Previously, he served as director and chair of Duke's Sanford Institute of Public Policy, and he has been a visiting scholar at the Kennedy School of Government at Harvard University. He has served as a consultant to the U.S. Department of Justice (Criminal Division) and the U.S. Department of the Treasury (Enforcement Division). He has published on a wide range of topics, including punishment, deterrence of crime, the costs of crime, homicide and economic conditions, and the epidemic in youth violence of the late 1980s and early 1990s. His other research interests include evaluation methods; public health policy; and the regulation of alcohol, guns, and gambling. He is a member of the Institute of Medicine. He holds a Ph.D. in economics from the University of California at Berkeley.

Steven N. Durlauf is the Kenneth J. Arrow and Laurents R. Christensen professor of economics at the University of Wisconsin–Madison and a research associate of the National Bureau of Economic Research. Previously, he served as director of the economics program at the Santa Fe Institute and as general editor of the revised edition of the *New Palgrave Dictionary of Economics*. His primary research interests involve the integration of the social influences into the theoretical and statistical analysis of economic phenomena, and he has also studied issues related to racial profiling, deterrence and imprisonment, and deterrence and death penalty. He is a fellow of the Econometric Society. He holds a Ph.D. in economics from Yale University.

Amelia M. Haviland holds the Anna Loomis McCandless chair at the Heinz College at Carnegie Mellon University, and she is a senior statistician at RAND. Her research focuses on causal analysis with observational data and analysis of longitudinal and complex survey data with applications in health, criminology, and economics. Her methodological work has included new methods to combine semi-parametric mixture modeling for longitudinal data with propensity score approaches to causal modeling and methods for creating minimum mean squared error composite estimates from a combination of probability and nonprobability samples. She is a recipient of the Thomas Lord Scholarship Award from the RAND Institute for Civil Justice. She holds a Ph.D. in statistics and public policy from Carnegie Mellon University.

Gerard E. Lynch is a judge on the U.S. Court of Appeals for the Second Circuit, and he is the Paul J. Kellner professor of law at the Columbia University School of Law. Previously, he served on the U.S. District Court for the Southern District of New York. Prior to his appointment to the bench, he served as vice dean of the Columbia University School of Law. His main areas of expertise include sentencing and criminal law and procedure. He is a recipient of the Edward Weinfeld Award for Distinguished Contributions to the Administration of Justice from the New York County Lawyers' Association and of the Wien Prize for Social Responsibility from Columbia University. He holds degrees from Columbia College and the Columbia University School of Law.

Charles F. Manski is a Board of Trustees professor in economics at Northwestern University. Previously, he served on the faculties of the University of Wisconsin–Madison, the Hebrew University of Jerusalem, and Carnegie Mellon University. His research spans econometrics, judgment and decision, and the analysis of social policy. He is an elected member of the National Academy of Sciences and an elected fellow of the Econometric Society, the American Academy of Arts and Sciences, and the American Association for the Advancement of Science. He holds a B.S. and a Ph.D. in economics from the Massachusetts Institute of Technology.

John V. Pepper is associate professor of economics at the University of Virginia. His research focuses on program evaluation methods, applied econometrics, and public economics. He has published widely on a range of topics, including evaluation of criminal justice data and programs, food assistance programs, health and disability programs, and welfare programs. He is on the board of the Michigan Retirement Research Center and of the Southern Economics Association. He is a coeditor of the *Southern Economic Journal*, and he served as a guest editor for a special issue of the *American Journal of Law and Economics*, which focused on empirical research on the death penalty. He holds a Ph.D. in economics from the University of Wisconsin–Madison.

James Q. Wilson was the Reagan professor of public policy at Pepperdine University and a distinguished scholar in the Department of Political Science and senior fellow at the Clough Center at Boston College. Previously, he was the Shattuck professor of government at Harvard University and the James Collins professor of management and public policy at the University of California at Los Angeles. His national positions related to issues of public policy included chair of the White House Task Force on Crime, chair of the National Advisory Commission on Drug Abuse Prevention, member of the Attorney General's Task Force on Violent Crime, member of the President's Foreign Intelligence Advisory Board, and member of the board of directors of the Police Foundation. He held a Ph.D. from the University of Chicago.